CHANGING WOMEN CHANGING CHURCH

CHANGING WOMEN CHANGING CHURCH

Festschrift to Patricia Brennan, M.B., B.S.
Foundation President of the Movement
for the Ordination of Women

Edited by Marie Louise Uhr

MILLENNIUM
BOOKS

First published in 1992 by
Millennium Books
an imprint of E.J. Dwyer (Australia) Pty Ltd
3/32–72 Alice Street
Newtown NSW 2042
Australia

National Library of Australia
Cataloguing-in-Publication data

Changing women, changing church : festschrift to Patricia Brennan ...

Includes bibliographical references.
ISBN 0 85574 909 1.

1. Women in Christianity. 2. Women clergy. I. Uhr, Marie Louise, 1935-   . II. Brennan, Patricia, 1928-

261.8344

Typeset in 11/13½pt Palatino by Post Typesetters
Printed in Australia by Macarthur Press.

Distributed in Ireland and the UK by:

Columba Book Service
93 The Rise
Mount Merrion
BLACKROCK CO. DUBLIN
Ph: (01) 283 2954
Fax: (01) 288 3770

ACKNOWLEDGEMENTS

I am deeply grateful to Catherine Hammond of Millennium Books for her patience, perseverance and wise guidance as I gathered together material for this festschrift.

My thanks too to copyright owners for permission to reproduce extracts used in this book:

to the Editor of St Mark's Review, Dr Graeme Garrett, St Mark's National Theology Centre, Canberra, for permission to use the article 'The Portrayal of Women in the Lectionary' from *St Mark's Review* 135, 22–25 (1988);

to Gwen Harwood and Publishers Collins/Angus & Robertson, Sydney, for permission to reproduce 'I am the Captain of my soul' from *Selected Poems*, by Gwen Harwood, 1990;

to Anne Elder and Collins/Angus & Robertson Publishers, Sydney, for permission to reprint two extracts from 'Crazy Woman', from *Crazy Woman and Other Poems* by Anne Elder, 1976;

to The Sisters of St Joseph and Fr Peter Malone, the Editor of *Compass, A Review of Topical Theology*, Chevalier Press, Kensington, NSW for permission to reprint the letter from Irene McCormack, RSJ, which appeared in *Compass, A Review of Topical Theology*, 25 (4) 33–35 (1991);

to Julia Macrae Books for 'The Third Thing' by D. H. Lawrence from *Birds, Beasts and the Third Thing* by D. H. Lawrence, Julia Macrae, London, 1982.

Every effort has been made to locate the sources of quoted material and to obtain authorisation for its use.

CONTENTS

About the Contributors

Veronica Brady is Senior Lecturer in English at the University of Western Australia and writes on questions of Australian literature, culture and film. Her most recent book is *The Crucible of Prophets: Australians and the Question of God*. She provides an articulate religious voice in Australian intellectual life.

Alison Cheek is an Australian who has lived for 38 years in America, making regular excursions back to Australia, often in some pastoral capacity to the women here who recognize her as a model for ministry. In 1974, as one of the Philadelphia Eleven, she was ordained priest in the Episcopal Church. She has worked as a teacher, a psychotherapist, a parish priest and a consultant for women in religion. Currently she is Director of Feminist Liberation Theology Studies at the Episcopal Divinity School in Cambridge, Massachusetts, USA.

Elisabeth Schüssler Fiorenza, an internationally renowned scholar, lecturer and teacher, combines scholarly work on biblical interpretation with pioneering research in feminist theology and hermeneutics. She was the first woman to be president of the Society of Biblical Literature, and has served on editorial boards of major biblical journals. She is an editor of *Religious Studies Review* and of *Concilium*. Together with Judith Plaskow, she has founded and edits *The Journal of Feminist Studies in Religion*. Her books, *In Memory of Her* and *Bread Not Stone* have been translated into several languages and have been widely acclaimed. Her most recent books are *Revelation: Vision of a Just World*, and, *But She Said*.

Janet and John Gaden met and married at Trinity College, University of Melbourne, where both studied Arts and John studied Theology. During 27 years of marriage they taught each other a lot; in the last years they wrote and taught together in dialogue form. As consultant theologian to three Archbishops of Melbourne and as secretary of the General Synod Doctrine Commission, John wrote on a wide range of issues, while teaching theology in the Melbourne and Adelaide Colleges of Divinity. He was an early and passionate advocate of women's ministries and ordination. We remember him with gratitude for sharing the restriction of women deacons de-barred from 'priestly functions'. Janet was the first moderator of the Movement for the Ordination of Women in Victoria and later a convenor in Adelaide and an editor of the National MOW Newsletter. She was ordained deacon in Adelaide in 1988. 'Calling God Names' was begun when John was Warden of St Barnabas College, Adelaide, and Janet was Deacon Assistant in the Adelaide parish of Hawthorn. It was finished some time after John's sudden death when Janet had become Deacon in charge of King Island, Tasmania, where she now lives with the youngest of their four children.

Roberta Hakendorf, IBVM, is a Loreto Sister who has been secondary school teacher, social worker and theology student. Her concern for social justice is finding new expression in exploring avenues to assist aboriginal people particularly with their education. She has long been a strong advocate of women's ministries and an active MOW member.

Janet Scarfe is President of the National Movement for the Ordination of Women in Australia; she succeeded Patricia Brennan as president in 1989.

John Shelby Spong has been bishop of Newark (New Jersey) since 1976. He has published widely and has been featured in television and radio programs around the world. Educated at the Virginia Theological Seminary, he has done graduate study at Union Seminary, Yale, Harvard and Oxford and has recently been a Quatracentenary Fellow at Cambridge University UK. His latest books are *Living in Sin? A Bishop Rethinks Human Sexuality*, and, *Rescuing the Bible from Fundamentalism*.

Marie Louise Uhr is Senior Lecturer in Biochemistry at the University of Canberra and has been an active member of both MOW and WATAC (Women and the Australian Catholic Church), including being a National Vice-President of MOW from '89 to '91.

Preface
Janet Scarfe

he name Patricia Brennan is for many Australians synonymous with the struggle for the ordination of women as deacons, priests and bishops in the Anglican Church. She has been both a prophetic voice herself and the inspirer of other prophetic women and men. At times together, at others individually, they have urged that Church to realise the full participation of women in the community of faith, so that the Church speaks of the equality of all in Christ, not only with its lips, but in its life.

Patricia has been a persistent disturber of the comfortably churched, insistent irritant to armchair ecclesiastical liberals, and strong comforter of those distressed by the Church's leaden reaction to the challenge of Christian feminism. Rarely, if ever, has she been content with the pace of change for women in the Church. And as if that did not cause some people enough consternation, she has always been immediately eager to explore the full implications of whatever positive changes have occurred, while others prefer to pause for self-congratulation, or even just breath.

This collection of essays has been prepared by some of Patricia's many friends, admirers, and companions along the way during the last decade. They are women and men, lay and ordained, from other Christian traditions as well as Anglican, from Australia and overseas. They view a map from their own distinctive perspectives. That map is the Church being challenged in the power of the Holy Spirit. The Movement for the Ordination of Women offers this book in celebration and thanksgiving for Patricia and all prophetic voices of Christian feminism in Australia and elsewhere.

During the 1970s, after considerable controversy and some acrimonious opposition, women were ordained to the priesthood in various parts of the Anglican communion, including Hong Kong, the United States, Canada, and New Zealand. In the late 1970s and early 1980s, growing numbers of lay people and clergy in Australia also pressed for the ordination of women, and for an end to all other expressions of the Church's entrenched sexism.[1]

The Movement for the Ordination of Women (MOW) emerged in Australia in 1983. Its name and to some extent the impetus for its formation came from the English Movement for the Ordination of Women, founded in 1979. Its real origins, however, were in the inspiration and commitment of already existing groups and individuals in a number of dioceses, such as the Women and Holy Orders in Adelaide. The establishment of the first branch in Sydney was followed quickly by the formation of branches in Adelaide, Melbourne, Perth, Brisbane and Canberra. These came together as the first members of the national Movement for the Ordination of Women, with Patricia Brennan as president. Since then, MOW branches have been formed in Armidale, Bendigo and Ballarat, and strong contacts established elsewhere.

MOW's name suggests commitment to one issue only, the ordination of women to the three-fold order of deacon, priest and bishop. In reality, we in MOW see this as a symbol for a much broader issue—the way the Church regards all women, both in its own community of faith and the community at large. Since its earliest days, with Patricia as president, MOW has also striven:

- To encourage women to hear and respond to the call of God.
- To recognise, encourage and extend the ministries of women, and to see that the Church makes full use of them.
- To express women's perspectives in theology, to celebrate their diversity of spirituality, and to promote the use of inclusive language in worship.
- To bring laity and clergy into closer partnership.
- To liaise with appropriate national and international women's groups.

From its beginnings MOW has been a strong and very public stimulus for debate about both the ordination of women in the Anglican Church and the broader issue of women in religious institutions and in religious thought. Various positive changes in the Church regarding the nature, role and contributions of women since the 1980s are, in fact, in sympathy with our aims. These changes are increasingly evident in almost

3

every aspect of church life — language, liturgy, theology, participation in decision-making, and the clergy.[2]

MOW has been instrumental in what is a revolution in the Church and almost every aspect of its life. We have raised the Church's consciousness, explored and spoken out about new areas of theology, and with very mixed feelings found our way into the Church's decision-making processes. We have been and will continue to be a vital component of the debate and change. In some dioceses, the changes apparent elsewhere are still most vigorously resisted, and MOW provides a much-needed forum for debate, exploration and challenge, as well as for mutual support and pastoral care for like-minded women and men. In other dioceses, where changes in the role of women appear on the surface to have been more welcomed and supported, MOW continues to challenge their pace and extent, and to explore their fuller dimensions.

Change is more obvious than continuity, however. Not one of those changes has come easily. That changes are occurring should not overshadow the determined persistence of sexism in the Church, or veil the ugliness of opposition and the compromising of liberals. Nor should it mean that the extent of the task and the courage required are underestimated.

Writing about MOW's early days, Patricia has reflected on the magnitude of the task:

> When those who come after us go looking through the evidence of how it all began, they will wonder at the absence of the names of the first editors of the MOW Magazine, the disjointed articles and the illustrations without signatures.
>
> I think, looking back, we left them out because what we were doing frightened us. From our kitchens and our studies, by telephone and word processor, most with children at our skirts, we were taking on no less than the power of the patriarchal Church. We weren't the first, and we shan't be the last.
>
> To have gone to the press and onto the streets and declared publicly in front of our cathedrals that a great

4

wrong was being done to women in the Church, put our hearts into our mouths. But, in the prophetic tradition, it isn't a bad place for the heart to be kept.[3]

Patricia's pioneering and prophetic stance has not, however, been confined to either the Anglican Church or Australia. The Christian feminist movement within the Australian Church has long had firm connections with Christian feminists overseas, particularly those from the Anglican and Catholic traditions. Contacts have flourished across oceans and continents. The Rev. Dr Alison Cheek, an Australian living in the United States who was one of the 'Philadelphia Eleven' ordained in 1974,[4] has been a close friend of Patricia and others in the Movement for some years. She has also visited Australia regularly at key times of decision in the Anglican Church, such as the General Synods of 1987 and 1989. Such contacts have given the issue an additional dimension, and prevented it from being discussed solely in parochial terms.

Throughout her period as leader of MOW and no less since, Patricia has worked hard with others to set the debate in Australia within a far broader context than gender balance among clergy in the Anglican Church. Her determination to establish and draw on both international and ecumenical contacts have added a great richness to the issue, a richness whose impact is just beginning to be felt by the institutional Church but which is very strong on its fringes.

Illustrations abound of Patricia's commitment to Australian Anglicanism's participation in significant world-wide social and theological debates. In 1988, she led a delegation of Australian women to the Lambeth Conference of Bishops, where they joined others from fifteen countries around the Anglican communion. Together as the Women's Witnessing Community they drew attention to the urgency of questions facing women in Church and society. In February, 1989, she attended and reported widely through the media on the consecration of the first woman bishop in the Anglican communion, the Right Reverend Barbara Harris, suffragan (assistant) bishop of Massachusetts. Among those she has interviewed are Archbishop

5

Desmond Tutu (an exclusive interview for the ABC on his visit to Australia in 1987), the controversial bishops David Jenkins and Jack Spong, and equally controversial Cambridge theologian Don Cupitt.

The Movement's national annual conferences have also provided opportunities to see the Australian experience within a wider Christian context. Since 1985, the conference has been a forum for the exchange of women's experiences, ideas, and soundings in liturgy, biblical exegesis and history. From the first, international as well as Australian contributions have participated.[5]

In 1989, the National MOW Conference became ecumenical as well as international. It was a bold move, and sprang from Patricia's international contacts and travels.

The conference 'Towards a Feminist Theology' attracted some 450 women and men, and a second ecumenical conference, 'Women Authoring Theology', was held in 1991.

Recognition

Patricia's contribution to the transformation of the Church has already been acknowledged in several significant ways. In 1988, the bicentennial year of white settlement in Australia, Patricia was one of ten recipients of the prestigious *Women 88* awards. There were 1200 nominations from all parts of Australia, from which a panel of prominent women selected the award winners. Patricia's award was for services to women in religion and health.

The Women of Faith Calendar, published by the Australian Council of Churches' Commission on the Status of Women to name women who have "committed their lives to a journey of religious, political and social justice issues", sets aside 10 January to honour Patricia as a "prophet in our time". Her achievements, with those of other women from many times and many places, "encourage and empower women of the twentieth century to maintain the struggle in faith within the Church in a society which continues to deny [the] full humanity and spirituality of women".

Patricia was appointed Feminist-in-Residence at the 1992 Deakin University Summer Institute of Women's Studies, as

6

well as presenter of a course in feminist theology—a key part of the Institute program.

The Movement for the Ordination has named her Foundation President of the Movement to acknowledge her unique and pioneering contribution to the transformation of the place of women in religion and society.

This *festschrift*, however, is the Movement's gift to Patricia Brennan, and to all women and men committed to transforming the Christian Church into the more just, equitable and compassionate community that the gospel demands.

In honouring Patricia, the Movement honours many. It honours all those in the Anglican Church who, with Patricia, have challenged their Church's self-righteous pronouncements and its self-satisfied silence on issues of justice for the excluded and marginalised. It honours those who, with Patricia, have crossed the walls that still exist between the institutional Churches, and found there a great company of like-minded women recovering our traditions, celebrating our past, stripping away centuries of neglect resulting from man-made prejudice and conceit. It honours those who travel, at great cost to body and spirit, to the formidable councils of the Church to contest the exclusivity of maleness and clericalism. It honours all those whose search for God through theology has not been defined or confined by traditional seminary conventions and curriculum, and who are articulating centuries of hidden experience.

It could be said, then, that the number it honours is growing rapidly and daily. It is a gift binding past, present and future, and we hope that it will be as enduring as Patricia's contribution to the transformation of the Church.

Janet Scarfe
National President
Movement for the Ordination of Women

---

1. *See Muriel Porter,* Women and the Church: The Great Ordination Debate, *Penguin, Ringwood, 1989.*
2. *By the end of 1991, nearly 150 women had been ordained deacon since 1986. They have worked in all but three of twenty-four Australian Anglican dioceses, including those which*

had expressed determined opposition to women in any of the three orders of ministry. One Australian woman who was ordained deacon and priest in the diocese of Newark, New Jersey, in 1988, is not recognised as a priest in Australia and is permitted a licence simply as a deacon.

3. In Movement for the Ordination of Women Newsletter, Winter 1989.

4. The 'Philadelphia Eleven' were eleven women ordained by three retired Episcopalian bishops in 1974.

5. List of speakers includes Janet and John Gaden, Veronica Brady, Alison Cotes, Bruce Rumbold.

Introduction
Marie Louise Uhr

❈

t seems appropriate to open this collection of essays with the words of Sister Veronica Brady, who has been a major speaker at several Movement for the Ordination of Women (MOW) conferences during which she inspired, challenged and strengthened us. Her essay in this book is based on a talk she gave at the 1987 conference, called "Crossing Over the Frontier". Her title, "The Shape of Stillness: Praying Over the Frontier", reminds us that, for many women interested in feminism and feminist theology, there comes a time when they realise that they have reached or have crossed a frontier, a boundary separating them from the comfortable place they used to be. They are now in an unknown country. This can be both frightening and exhilarating.

Veronica Brady describes three stages of this journey to the frontier. There is first the realisation of oppression, even in the Church which should be a sign of liberation; second, a positive call from God to let go of the known and safe, to go into the desert; and third, the encounter with the awesomeness of God, the thunder and lightning of Sinai. To make this journey, prayer must be the essence of our lives: listening to God is the critical act. And for us for whom it is an Australian journey, part of our listening must be to Australian voices speaking in prose, novels, poetry, art, and theology of the search, here, now, in this country, for "community with all those others who are wounded, whose worlds or lives also seem to be falling apart, yet who are actually—we must believe—giving birth to something new".

Our Judaeo-Christian story, which is both old and new, is always a story of setting out on pilgrimage, of wandering in the desert, of being called forward by prophets. Today we must find new prophets; I suspect that many of them will be women.

The words of the Anne Elder poem, "the magpie lark and the private lark", suggest that the larrikin element of Australians, the sense of play, of not taking ourselves too seriously, must be part of our journey even while we know that the issue is life and death.

Veronica Brady calls us to prayer, to a life of listening to God wherever God is found. Our next authors, Janet and John Gaden, write of the difficulties many women now find in speaking to God. Janet and John Gaden have been moving, stirring, and shaping figures in MOW since its beginning, and the tragedy of John's sudden death early in 1990 was felt by many throughout Australia. It is with great joy, therefore, that we are able to preserve something of his thought here.

In "Calling God Names", Janet is, as usual, direct and searingly honest: how do we talk to this God we find in the desert? She first considers the use of 'Father', the name most often used in Church liturgy. This, she points out, makes God responsible for half of her being, whereas God is source of all.

Her clear statement of this reminds us that until recently, biological science has believed the father to be the prime source of the creation of the child. The mother was thought to supply nutrients—the ovum was a container of food (another version of the female as the great nurturer)—while the male sperm contained the force and form for the child. Aristotle not only clearly stated the thought of his time, but by the force of his intellect persuaded future generations to the truth of his claims. As Nancy Tuana has written, "He believed that the male imparts to the female the form of the fetus. The female role in reproduction is to provide the material, the menstrual blood, upon which the male semen imparts form. The female body thus becomes the workplace and source of raw material out of which the male crafts a human life".[1]

With this biological understanding, it made sense to see the creator God as father. The God of Genesis breathed upon the dust of the earth and created life; and the seed of the male is the power which creates the form and nature of a human being from the blood of a woman's womb. God is acting as fathers act. Aristotelian biology remained authoritative for many centuries, accepted scientifically and theologically, and was restated and given new theological force by Thomas Aquinas, who compared the generation of humans to that of the creation of the world. As God alone produces form in matter, so the active seminal power of man's seed gives form to the corporeal matter supplied by the mother. In spite of over a

11

thousand years of detailed and careful anatomical work by Galen and other anatomists, the beliefs of Aristotle and his confrères held sway, so that all anatomical insights were understood through Aristotelian theory.

The advent of the microscope provided a new tool for accurate scientific work on the details of human reproduction, but not surprisingly, what was viewed through the microscope was understood in terms of current scientific theories, so that current beliefs determined what was seen. Antony van Leeuwenhoek (1632–1723) 'saw' what he called *spermatic animalcules* under the microscope when he looked at sperm: i.e., he thought he saw a tiny person in the sperm cells. This theory of generation became known as the preformation theory because it stated that humans existed preformed in the male sperm cells, and these little people grew when they were inserted into the womb and nurtured by the female. This did not challenge the earlier belief, therefore, that the male created the child and the female was merely the nurturer. The acceptance of this preformation theory, in spite of logical difficulties (such as what happens to all the 'little people' who do not enter an egg) survived until the nineteenth century, giving continuing support to the belief in a male god as the great creator. Even with understandings of the fusion of chromosomes from male and female egg cells to form the new embryo, the male was still given the active part. Only with the advent of the electron microscope is the activity of the ovum becoming recognised.

Now that we are aware that both partners contribute equally to the offspring (or rather that the mother contributes just a little bit more, as she contributes the DNA of the mitochondria with its own small genome) it is time to put aside our belief in the male as the great creator and accept that as human creation requires both male and female, so also both male and female images are required to give human representation to the creative power of God. While it is easy to see why the term 'Father' became such a powerful term for God when people believed that fathers created children, now that we understand the poor biology on which this belief rests, surely it is time to let go of this image of father as the great divine image.

While some women are finding strength in the use of the name 'Mother' for God, Janet rejects it too because it implies only a partial power of creation. Instead, she finds strength in terms such as 'friend' and 'lover' for the God she knows best as the silent companion God. The God she knows is the God who walks beside her, and who sits with her as she sits in prayer. It is also the God she finds in other people, the incarnate God, the God who is found in relationships, whom Carter Heyward calls "the power in right relation".[2] It is, Janet finds, particularly in silence that we commune, "in silence we reach a deeper relation than one to one, like lovers who 'are one'". This leads her to the difficult question: is God someone who relates to us, or is God 'relating' itself? Are you, she writes to God, an entity? She answers in the negative, but puzzles even more as to *how* can we address God, while knowing that we do and we always have done so.

Janet first wrote her letter to God in 1988 and gave a copy to John, who wrote to her commenting on how he was fascinated by her "holding embodied relationships together with the way of silence". In this he saw her combining two areas of spirituality which traditional Christianity has always kept separate: the silent communing of the soul alone with God, and the belief in the incarnate God found in relationships with others. He asked her to elaborate on this.

After John's sudden and tragic death, Janet has tried to do this. Struggling with words, which reach into the silence, she tries to push her understanding of the tension between relationships and silence. The experience of John's death has taught her, at a terrible price, the presence of God in the silent physical presence of another, even, or perhaps especially in this case, of another in death. In this section, Janet embodies for me the vulnerable God as she shares with the unknown reader something of the pain of John's death and of God's place for her in that.

Janet Gaden begins to open up new images of our mysterious God and help us to let go of outdated, no longer valid names. The image of God these names portray is one of the critical issues for women who choose to stay in the institutional

Church: our next contributor, Bishop Spong, sets out clearly why this is so.

The Rt Rev. John S. Spong, Bishop of the Episcopal Church in the Diocese of Newark, USA, an outspoken critic of the Church especially for its traditional positions on sexuality, has called his paper, "Women: Less Than Free in Christ's Church". In this essay, he discusses attitudes towards women in Church teachings, with particular emphasis on the aberrant sexuality of those pronouncements dealing with women and/or sexual relationships, over the whole 2000 years.

A very detailed history and critique of the Church's statements and treatment of women and sexuality has been given recently by Uta Ranke-Heinemann in *Eunuchs for Heaven: The Catholic Church and Sexuality*.[3] It is good to have a short and sharp summary of similar material here, especially written by one in a position of authority in the Church. Through his analysis of centuries of abuse against women and disparagement of sexuality and the body, he concludes that if the churches do not alter their attitudes to human sexuality but continue with their present sexual stereotyping, they are likely to become "an antiquated group of guerilla fighters isolated in forgotten pockets wondering why they are ignored and asking what happened to their cause". And with a ringing cry for change and a new and different outlook, he writes, "I cast my vote for a dangerous future". Would that all bishops would do likewise!

The effects of the misogyny of the Church, as summarised by Bishop Spong, are myriad, and tomes have been and could be written on them. As one small example of the way in which patriarchal structures impinge on the worshipping lives of women, we have included a paper analysing the lectionary still used in Anglican and Catholic churches in Australia to examine the pictures of women it portrays and models of women's lives it holds up to Australian women. The picture is bleak. Women are wives and mothers of sons or they are nothing at all. And the voices of women of scripture are barely heard in the churches. Through this silence and emphasis on maternity as a woman's only function, powerful messages are given to women and men that salvation history is the story

14

of the actions of great men whom women have quietly supported and nurtured, so that it is right and fitting that men should be our Church leaders today.

The effects of this hierarchical, male, clerical system on women are clear, but the way forward is not. It is important, then, to examine how we got where we are, because an examination of our history can often help to free us. Sister Roberta Hakendorf, IBVM, a staunch supporter of MOW for many years, writes on the origin and development of the priesthood in the Roman Catholic Church. The development of hierarchical government and the priesthood as a separate caste, which is still upheld by ecclesial authority, has depended on and been supported by a positivist interpretation of selected passages of scripture. The problems it causes are clearly seen. Strong opposition to the ordination of women is still evident in the Anglican Church, but the problems in the Catholic Church are even worse because the Catholic priesthood is not only all male but is celibate as well. Moreover, Western Catholicism is facing a crisis because there is a rapidly decreasing number of vocations to this male celibate priesthood. Parishes are getting larger; priestless Sundays are coming in; Eucharist is going out.

Nevertheless the hierarchy continues to maintain that only celibate males can be priests. The hierarchy calls for more vocations; it does not discuss a change in the system. It seems to me that there is a clear clash of values here. On the one hand it is said that an ordained priest is essential for Eucharist—only a priest can say the words of consecration—and that Eucharist is central to Christian community; on the other hand it is said that it is necessary, even if sad, to deny people regular Eucharist because there is a shortage of celibate males willing to be ordained. The two values are in conflict: on the one hand, the value of Eucharist, on the other the value of a male, celibate clergy. The Hierarchy of the Roman Catholic Church has made its values clearly known: the preservation of a male, celibate clergy is more important than Eucharist for the people.

In the face of this extraordinary decision, Roberta's examination of the evolution and ascendancy of a clerical caste is timely. Neither priest nor bishop was present in Jesus' time

15

or in Paul's Corinthian church. Presbyters operated in Jerusalem, while bishops and deacons were found at the time of the Pastoral Epistles, but none of these was considered a 'priest', a word that was not used until the middle of the second century. Over the centuries, we find increasing separation of clergy from laity, increasing development of a church architecture reinforcing this separation, increasing power of clergy over the spiritual well-being of the laity, increasing control over the liturgy and sacraments, increasing 'monoformity' of ministries.

Roberta sees hope for the future in an equal ministry of women and men working in base communities, such as those which have sprung up in South America, and she is afire with dreams of a real Church built of communities in communion. But first, the all-male hierarchical system, will have to go.

If this hierarchical priestly caste has been built largely on a positivist reading of certain passages of scripture, the way forward requires scholarly analyses of scripture to challenge these readings. No one has done more to challenge the traditional interpretations of the New Testament than Professor Elisabeth Schüssler Fiorenza.

Elisabeth Schüssler Fiorenza is Stendhal Professor of Divinity at Harvard Divinity School. She was to have been, at Patricia Brennan's invitation, the principal speaker at the first Australian ecumenical feminist theology conference, held in Sydney in 1989; illness prevented her appearance but she has remained a powerful supporter of feminist theology in Australia. She has chosen to write on "The Twelve and the Discipleship of Equals". The image of 'the Twelve' as Jesus' chosen leaders of an ordained male ministry has been critical to arguments against the ordination of women. For example, the Declaration on the Admission of Women to the Ministerial Priesthood given by the Sacred Congregation for the Doctrine of the Faith in 1976 states clearly that "Jesus Christ did not call any woman to become part of the Twelve", and then argues that the Twelve were the chosen founders of apostolic ministry. Hence, by this theory, an hierarchically-ordered, male ministry is of divine command and cannot be challenged without challenging the mind of God.

Elizabeth carefully and methodically analyses the evidence

in scripture, beginning with Corinthians 15:5, then with Matthew, Mark and Luke-Acts. Corinthians appears to speak of 'the Twelve' and the apostles as two different groups, while the oldest text in Matthew uses 'the Twelve' as an eschatological symbol, not as a reference to the historical apostles. Mark places 'the Twelve' among the disciples and gives them the specific power of exorcism and healing: this was their task. They are members of the disciples, many of whom preach, but Jesus is the preacher. Mark is concerned with the meaning of discipleship, and he shows that it is not 'the Twelve' but the women disciples who prove to be the true disciples.

It is Luke-Acts which identifies 'the Twelve' with the apostles and it is this identification which has been critical for the theology of apostolic succession; but an analysis of Luke-Acts shows that the apostles have a very limited post-resurrection function, disappearing before the end of the book. They are certainly not equated with leadership in the early Church and are not replaced. Their historical and symbolic function was not continued in the ministries of the Church—so we hear nothing of them in the Pastoral Epistles. Reminding us that the Gospels are theological responses to particular historical-ecclesial situations, Elizabeth continues to question traditional interpretations of early Christian documents and to open up possibilities of new readings. She challenges received meanings and the present power structures which use these interpretations for support. The twelve apostles had no successors. How can we, then, continue today to support the theological construct of apostolic succession?

The impressive scholarship of Elisabeth Schüssler Fiorenza begins to show us a way out of our present dilemmas. Detailed, careful, scholarly work is essential. And the fruits of this work must inform the syllabus of theological education. Alison Cheek writes of the feminist liberation theology seminary training at the Episcopal Divinity School of Boston, where they are aware that only by changing the theological education of both laity and clergy will changes occur in the churches.

Alison writes of the development of this feminist liberation theology, of her coming to see this as the way forward for her, of learning to do power analysis of social and Church structures, asking all the time: in whose interests is this custom? Who does this etiquette serve? Who benefits by this norm? Who is protected by this law? Who is being silenced? Who is being marginalised? Whose reality is being trivialised? Whose life is being forfeited?

Feminist liberation theology is a movement for change from all sexist, racist and classist structures. At Episcopal Divinity School they have learned that such theology can only be done in mixed classes, with at least several students of colour to provide a critical mass. Both privilege and oppression need to be analysed, and people must work from the starting point of personal experiences to the larger framework of society. Such analyses of the effects of class, race and sex on the curriculum and pedagogy of theological education are critically important for theological education in Australia right now as we begin to hear Aboriginal Australians and take our place in Asian conversations.

For many Australians and Asians, colonial oppression has left deep scars, so that racial power structures are much more important than sexist ones. White middle-class Australians have to learn to hear these voices in their midst.

There is much work to be done in Australia, and there are many women ready and willing to do it. As a final section of this book in honour of Patricia Brennan, we have gathered together a few examples of the writings of women who share Patricia's vision of a new Church. Most of the contributions to this last section are from the National MOW magazine, a newsletter/magazine which has come out several times a year since MOW began. In it many women have expressed their hopes and dreams. We have chosen a selection in which women reflect on God, our scriptures, our power and our Eucharist; it includes, as well as selections from MOW writings, an interview with Sister Angela of Stroud and a letter from Sister Irene McCormack, RSJ.

Because God is the central fact of existence for all contributors, we start with a short statement about the presence of God. Jean Groves is a biologist and her biological understanding is central to her thought. If we hold our breath we do not get more oxygen, we do not hold on to that air, we suffocate; so, she suggests, if we try to hold on to the presence of God, we lose God. Too rarely, I believe, do we use an understanding of our bodies to understand the God who made us. Spirituality has emphasised the supernatural. Perhaps feminist theology can help to emphasise the natural—not just nature out there—but our bodies as images of God.

Feminist thinking, too, as we have shown with the writings of Elisabeth Schüssler Fiorenza, is re-analysing scriptures. Peta Sherlock has taken a long look at Lot's wife, and seen new strengths and virtues in her. Traditional theology makes her a figure of disobedience—and are we surprised that it is the woman in the story who disobeys? After all so does Eve. But Peta hears Jesus' words about the virtue of salt and ties the two together for our enlightenment.

Alison Cheek also has looked hard and long at scripture and its picture of women. Listening afresh to the strictures against women in the epistles, women have begun to ask the question: why did they spend so much effort on this issue? Does not this mean that women were active at the time? Who bothers to make rulings against something which no one is doing and no one is even contemplating? We only make rules to stop something which some people are doing.

With a lively use of imagination, Alison has written a letter from Eunice to the Philippians. As she writes in her essay on teaching feminist liberation theology, in her work for a doctorate of ministry she considered "ways in which imagination may be used in breaking open old thought forms and opening up the possibility of new ways of thinking", using Schüssler Fiorenza's fourfold hermeneutical model as a way of entry. This letter is an example of such work. It highlights the spirited and powerful women who must have been in the community at the time that 1 Timothy was written and the struggles which they must have undergone. Not unlike our own.

Our struggles are with a highly institutionalised Church. Eileen Baldry, considering the Church as community, gathers reasons for people to stay in the institution and try to change it, but is very aware of all the societal reasons why this is so difficult. One group who must find it incredibly difficult to stay are homosexuals. Ali Wurm reminds us that it is not only women who are marginalised in the Church. Indeed the attitude to homosexuals is far worse. She concludes that "it is vital that we... express our full acceptance of homosexuals if we are to be a truly loving Church".

One branch of feminism assumes that if only women were in authority, all would be new and beautiful. But, as Heather Thomson's gentle parable illuminates, women are often the last to trust and affirm other women. This is not surprising. We have been taught and taught well that only men have magic powers, can be ordained, should be in authority. It is hard for many women to accept their own and other women's power.

The life and work of Sister Angela demonstrates women's spirituality and power, albeit in a traditional mould. Angela and her sisters, of the Anglican community of St Clare, built their monastery themselves, in Stroud, NSW, making their own mud bricks, and turned thirty acres of ridge and stone into beautiful orchards. Angela embodies intrepid female creativity. Elaine Lindsay interviewed Sister Angela for us. It seemed important to capture something of her spirit here because without her love, prayer and support, many MOW workers would have collapsed by the wayside. Dedicated religious women have always demonstrated to the world—if it wanted to see—the spirit, mind and soul of women in charge of their own affairs; women as leaders of communities; women as theologians; women as labourers and gardeners. Now as Anglican women deacons, unable yet to be ordained, and Catholic sisters, for whom ordination is not even yet an option, run parishes here and overseas, we begin to see the absurdity of the present system. Churches are still arguing whether or not it is in the mind of God to allow women to be in positions of authority, especially spiritual authority, and yet all around us it is happening. All around us women are quietly assuming their rightful place, often because men cannot be found to be there. Yet these women are still denied official recognition of their ministry, still denied the right to celebrate the Eucharist.

Sister Irene McCormack, RSJ, who was murdered by terrorists in Peru, where she was working, summed it up in a letter she wrote not long before she died, as only an Australian could: "It seems to me, therefore," she writes, "that the preoccupation of our Church leaders with power and control over who can celebrate the Eucharist, who can and who can't receive the Eucharist, is right up the creek". It could not be better said. There is nothing more to say.

Marie Louise Uhr
National Vice-President
Movement for the Ordination of Women

1. Nancy Tuana, 'The Weaker Seed: The Sexist Bias of Reproductive Theory', in Feminism and Science, ed. Nancy Tuana, Indiana University Press, Bloomington, 1989.
2. Carter Heyward, Touching our Strength, Harper & Row, San Francisco, 1989, and earlier works.
3. Uta Ranke-Heinemann, Eunuchs for Heaven: The Catholic Church and Sexuality, Andre Deutsch, London, 1990.

The Shape of Stillness:
Praying over the Frontier
Veronica Brady

here is a sense, I think, in which many women in the Church today feel themselves to be on the frontier, on some kind of boundary between the known and the unknown; between order, custom, and the grace and ease of habit and a feeling of darkness, confusion, doubt and anxiety. This is the feeling generated by moving out into strange new country, moving out into territory as yet unmapped. Yet in another sense, this feeling or at least this situation is the proper, even the normal, one for Christians. We are by definition a pilgrim people, called always beyond our certainties to explore ever more fully the mystery of the "realities at present unseen" which are for us the crucial realities. But it is also perhaps a situation characteristically Australian, whether we be non-Aboriginal people come into a strange, new country, "wanderer(s) on the way to the self" or Aboriginal people whose lives centre on the mysterious but potent presence in their midst which they call the 'Dreaming'.

What I would like to do first of all, therefore, is to spend some time on this notion of the journey, of moving across the frontier, because it seems to me that this is the notion which will enable us to make sense of our lives in general and of our present situation in particular. Let us take as our text a passage from one of Kafka's parables. "Where are you going to, master?" the passage begins, to which the reply is, "Away from here, anywhere, but away from here."

"So," he said, "so you know your destination?"

"Yes, didn't you hear me? It's away from here. My destination is away from here."[1]

"Anywhere, but away from here", that seems to me to be an important element in any story of change, but especially in the story of women in the Church, a story which has to do on the one hand with a great dissatisfaction with our present definitions of value and purpose, as well as with the present order of the Church; and on the other with a great longing for something more, for some place or way of being in which facts and values are not at odds but in harmony with one another, where the human and the spiritual are not the opposite of the real or the practical.

I think we can see something of this exemplified in the story of Ruth. After the death of her husband, first of all, and then of her sons, Ruth's mother-in-law Naomi, you will remember, decided to return home to her own country. Her two daughters-in-law, Ruth and Orpah, went with her. But when they reached the frontier, Naomi said goodbye, bidding them return to their own mothers. Naomi turned to go, but Ruth refused to move.

> *"Do not press me to leave you and to stop going with you, for wherever you go, I shall go, wherever you live, I shall live. Your people will be my people and your God will be my God. Where you die, I shall die and there I shall be buried. Let Yahweh bring unnameable ills on me and worse ills, too, if anything but death should part me from you!"*[2]

At the moment, there may be a particular appositeness in the story for those of us who are Roman Catholics as we watch those of you who are Anglicans move closer to the frontier, preparing for the crossing involved in being admitted to the ordained priesthood. Many of us are saying, if not "Let us go with you", at least, "we shall be with you".

But it applies more generally, to the fact that what impels us to the frontier and to the crossing is not ambition, not hunger for power, but the logic of love, the desire to move even more deeply into the mystery of love and service which is the mystery of the Christian God. It is also a mystery of diminishment: "If you would go to the All, you must go by a way in which you have nothing" (St John of the Cross). For the fact is that there is no external road to this goal which lies at the heart of who and what we are and long to be. There are no maps, because the goal is what Is, the mysterious one whose name is the unnameable and the unspeakable one who is love.

That brings us, then, to our title, 'The Shape of Stillness.' Our best guide to the unseen and unknown is listening, listening to what is being spoken to us here and now, on the frontier in the time before the crossing, in the kind of no-woman's land in which we find ourselves. What do we have to listen to? It is, I suggest, what we have: our apprehension and our anxiety.

If it is true that, as Schillebeeckx puts it, "the hermeneutical principle for the disclosure of reality is the scandal, the stumbling block",[3] then our problems can also be the occasions of grace. Truth for the Christian is marked by the sign of the cross and, in a sense, is the cross. The desert, literally or metaphorically, may therefore be the special place of God's speaking and coming towards us.

The story of Ruth is part, therefore, of that larger story, central to the Judaeo-Christian tradition, the Exodus, and therefore also the story of all who see themselves as people on the way.

This story, of course, begins with affliction, with the oppression of God's people by the Egyptians. It was important if they were to move forward, into the destiny God placed before them to make their own, for them to realise, first of all, that they were oppressed; and then that Pharaoh, the authority, was the source of their oppression, realizing, therefore, that power and goodness are not necessarily to be identified with authority—even, we might suggest, in the Church. What is provided here and now, the "onions and leeks of Egypt", is not, it seems, what matters most. Certainly here, it is in the sense of being oppressed, of feeling powerless, which provides the occasion for God's call. In the present instance, as far as women in the Church today are concerned, this feeling may well be the occasion not only to be aware of God but to broaden our compassion, to be aware, beyond our own relatively privileged plight, of all the others throughout the world who are subject to oppression of far worse kinds, of all the others who are grieving, often for much more terrible losses, and join, with them, in discovering the God whose special predilection is for "the little ones".

But—to continue the story—in the midst of that oppression, a child, Moses, a sign of new hope, is born, and lives because of the courage and solidarity of women. Egyptian law had it that every male child born to the people of Israel had to be put to death. But a group of women, including even a daughter of Pharaoh, one of the privileged, disobey that law, separating obedience to the law of Pharaoh from obedience to the law of God. Catching a glimpse of a different future and believing in it, they made a gesture of love and compassion, and it was this gesture which, saving the life of Moses, God's person, the liberator, made possible the liberation of the whole people. They were not prepared to accept that Pharaoh's rule would prevail forever and were prepared to challenge it, if not openly, at least effectively, risking themselves in the process.

The next stage is the positive 'call'. We have a good deal to learn, I think, from Moses. He did not take the call upon himself; his decision was not in a sense his own choice. He was the one who was chosen to bring about change, to liberate his people—men as well as women. It was because he was called—gifted by God—that he had not only the vision but the courage to fulfil it.

Nothing really effective for God takes place without this touch of God, without the glimpse of another kind of logic and power; Moses learned this in his vision of the burning bush, which was burning but never consumed—something not merely beyond our understanding but which challenges it.

Here, then, was the first frontier he had to cross, a frontier of understanding and thus of control. Moses had to let go, let God's logic prevail, and trust in God's love for his people which seemed to be asking him to do the impossible. The Judaeo-Christian God is the one who is always intent on leading us into new country. He will not let us stay still, being a God who is life and movement and promise, the source of our energy as well as of our hope.

In the present context, in which our need is for conciliation, not contestation, it may be well to pass over the next stage of the struggles to make the break from Egypt: the battles with Pharaoh, his opposition, his bullying, his changes of mind and the various plagues that were sent to punish him.

Let us move instead to the stage of the desert. When they passed over the frontier, when they left Egypt, the people of Israel did not go out into easy or fertile country. They found themselves in the desert, in what seemed a place of desolation, without most of the things they regarded not only as pleasant

but also necessary. Above all, they felt very much alone, sus-
pended between what had been and what was not yet—as
many women in the Church feel themselves today. But their
confidence, and ours, is surely that the place in which they
find themselves was not in the first instance the result of their
own choice, was not a response to merely social factors, but
a response to God's call. It was God who called them—and
us—out, away from their previous certainties, to be here. We
are going where God bids us go, doing what God bids us do—
at lease we hope so.

What one needs most of all in the desert, however, is trust,
the readiness and ability to wait, trusting that we shall find
manna, just enough for each day, and water even from a rock.
But for us, as for the Israelites, the temptation is to look back-
wards, to mourn lost comforts and certainties, as the Israelites
mourned the "onions and leeks" of Egypt. But the God who
calls us is often not comfortable; what he offers instead is
himself. On the way, though, we need to cherish one another,
share what we have and live simply, day by day, trusting that
what we need will be provided as it was for the people of
old. Then, finally, in the midst of the desert, there will be the
Sinai experience, the thunder and lightning.

This encounter with the awesomeness of God is perhaps
the most important stage of all. I suspect that what we women
in the Church need most at the moment is to think a great
deal more about 'spirituality', about prayer. With all that we
have had to do and say, we have perhaps sometimes lost sight
of this encounter, this central experience of our faith and hope
and love, the meeting with the God who is Other—not just
a mirror reflection of ourselves but the Other who is the ultimate
partner, the goal of all our loves. This God is love—of course—
but also, as the Sinai experience shows, terror, the kind of
experience expressed, for instance, in Blake's 'The Tyger', especially in the wonderful opening lines:

Tyger, tyger, burning bright
In the forests of the night

It seems to me that women's experience is often of this
kind, anyway. In birth especially, but also in the insistent and

intimate relationship women have with their bodies, power and sexuality and energy are caught up and fused, hammered out, if you like, in the furnace of creation. And that is also where God is, in this terrible, sometimes terrifying, even drunken, energy, just as much as in gentleness and serenity. The biblical God is not the God of the philosophers, a reasonable God who fits the calculations of the human mind. This God is or can be violent, urgent, transforming. Gwen Harwood understands something of this in her poem, 'I am the Captain of my Soul':

> But the Captain is drunk, and the crew
> hauling hard on his windlass of fury are whipped
> by his know-nothing rage. Their terror
> troubles the sunlight. 'Now tell me,'
> the Captain says, as his drunkenness
> drifts into tears, 'what's to keep me
> at ease in this harbour?'
>   'We'll tell you,'
> say Hands, 'in our headlong chase through a fugue
> for three voices, you heard a fourth voice naming
> divisions of silence. We'll summon
> that voice once again, it may tell you
> of marvels wrung from sorrows endured.'
> 'We have seen,' say Eyes, 'how in Venice
> the steps of churches open and close
> like marble fans under water.'
>
> 'You can rot in your sockets,' the Captain cries.
>
> 'I have children,' says Body, haloed
> in tenderness, firm in rightness still.
> 'I grew gross with their stress, I went spinning
> in a vortex of pain. I gave my breast
> and its beauty to nourish their heedless growth.
> They jump on my shoulder in mischievous joy.
> On their lives your astonishing sorrows
> flow easy as water on marble steps.'
>
> 'Lass sie betteln gehn,' roars the Captain

29

as his old wounds burn, and he gulps
from his flagon of grief. 'You servants, you things,
stand up there! You with the ageing choir-boy face,
and you with your facile dexterity, you
with your marble hallucinations, COME!'

Hands, eyes, body keel to the void as the drunken
Captain sings in his wilderness of water.[4]

Over the frontier, in the wilderness, it can seem as if the world is falling to pieces in this way, and yet the call keeps coming, a call, I think, which is not so much to power as to community with all those others who are wounded, whose worlds or lives also seem to be falling apart, yet who are actually—we must believe—giving birth to something new. In this country, this is truest perhaps of our Aboriginal sisters and brothers, but it is the case also with many others—young people, immigrants, old people—as well as women.

The desert, then, is a dangerous place. But it can also be exhilarating. We Church people in particular have been clinging to the fringes of self and of experience for too long. But now we begin to realise that we are out—to use another metaphor—'forty thousand fathoms deep', on the great ocean of being, open to "the heart pain, the world pain" (Conrad), as we were not perhaps before.

We need all of our strength in this situation, but that is, I believe, the strength which comes from powerlessness. In the past our great gift as women, painful as it may have been, has perhaps been this powerlessness. Power, as we know, corrupts very easily, can kill off certain sympathies and initiatives. But women mostly have been able to sit more easily by the wells of life, to know what it is to be solitary, less pressured to conform because less powerful socially, economically and politically. It is important not to move too far away from this solitude, from this inwardness which is the place of the living God and of prayer, to listen to the muse Anne Elder invokes in her poem, 'Crazy Woman', sitting

... musing under the lyric tree
plucking and plaiting the thoughtful branches
deep in the heart of the public gardens...[5]

What one learns is that there is a secret wisdom, something not much acknowledged in larger society, in the world of affairs or even, I am afraid, by the institutional Church. Indeed, this wisdom will sometimes seem crazy and must be expressed diffidently. Elder's poem knows this:

I debated how to say it aloud,
to their alarm. Before our death
there is much to communicate that goes by the board
because it is thought unusual indeed crazy
to gather the fallen leaf and the daisy,
the magpie lark and the private lark
in the public park,
the eternal cherubic spout, the nakedness
and lovingness of loneliness
into the right word
to bless our other selves in the name of the Lord.[6]

But this is our task: to be prayerful, to be strong, to be prophetic and to dance that prophecy, as it were, to shout for joy at what we have heard and seen, the promise of the Lord that we shall enter into even richer possibilities of love, worship and service—like Miriam shouting for joy after the passage through the Red Sea, and like so many of the other great women of the Judaeo-Christian tradition.

The source of this joy, however, is the notion of God, the "One who is Mighty" who has done such great things for, in and through us, who perhaps asks us to bring alive once more the true meaning of a word which has been obscured by so much misunderstanding, self-interest and cant, obscured sometimes by the Church which exists to proclaim it. It is for us to witness to the fact of this, the essential Word without which nothing else has meaning, and that is what our journey is about, the journey to the God who calls and who Is, the love which draws us, *"amor meus, pondus mea"* (St Augustine). The weight which draws me, the dynamic which empowers me, is the God who is the love through whom and in whom we are able to love ourselves in the first place and then others.

That is what we may call the ecstatic side of the equation. There is another side, however, and it is summed up in the image of the Crucified God. To love is to be vulnerable. But it is also to know oneself personally, not just the other, as vulnerable, because God's love goes out particularly to those who are wounded—that is the point of Matthew's parable of judgement,[7] the culmination of his series of parables of the Kingdom.

In this way, it therefore becomes possible to see God in the wounds inflicted upon us, often in the name of God, as we attempt to remain true to the liberator God we believe in. Some, perhaps many, of us have difficulty with the notion of Church at the moment. But if we think of it as the group of those called (*ecclesia*) out into the desert to live, in all our woundedness, we may be recovering a truer sense of Church than if we were to concentrate on institutional matters.

This community is called out to search for God, not to own God, but to have God as the one who goes before, at once guiding us and our goal. But, and this is our last point, this is a community not of the powerful or the important, not the winners but the little ones, people who often seem to ourselves and others to be foolish and to be failures. In our journey, as we look forward to the community of love, freedom and justice we believe in and hope for, it is important also to recover the great memory, enshrined not only in the story of the Exodus but also of the God who became the Poor Man of Nazareth. This, of course, is a memory of suffering, dangerous because counterfactual, a challenge to the false values of the world which crucified and goes on crucifying God.

At present I would argue that Australian society by and large worships false gods, an unholy trinity of Mammon (God of wealth and possessions), Moloch (God of struggle and ruthless competition) and Marilyn Monroe (emblem of the murderous power of the mindless search for pleasure and sensation). But this great memory contests their power and constitutes the revolution we are looking for, a revolution of values which works on the one hand to change the world for future generations and on the other unites us in the present with the whole suffering and wounded, joyous and loving community of God's people. In this view, the value of history is not to be found only or even especially in the successful, the conquerors. Its most important centre lies with those who might otherwise be called the losers, those who have managed to survive, who go on through the desert, hoping against hope.

What we really want and need, then, is God, to believe in God's call and to remain faithful to it. It is, of course, a long process—one of the significant elements of the Exodus story is that, in a sense, when God's people thought they had arrived in the promised land, they had not. You never really arrive there in this world, although in another sense you are always in it—so long as you are listening to God and thus learn that you must continue to move on because God is movement.

In the long run, therefore, it is a matter of perspective. The great English woman mystic of the fourteenth century, Julian of Norwich, had a glimpse of the perspective we need, I think, when she saw "all thing that are... as it were a little hazelnut in the Divine Hand." It was this vision which gave her the deep confidence that "all shall be well, and all manner of thing shall be well." But she also had a glimpse of God as Mother, a vision to balance the fierce God of the desert. Let us end, then, with this vision since the desert in which we find ourselves may thus be said to be an aspect of her kindness:

> *Thus, Jesus Christ, that Doeth good against evil, is our very Mother. We have our being with him, for there the ground of Motherhood begineth, with also the sweet keeping of love that endlessly followeth. As truly as God is our Father, so truly is God our Mother. That showeth He in all. And especially in those sweet words where he sayeth "I It Am". That is to say, I am the might and the goodness of Father God. I It Am, the wisdom and the kindliness of Mother God. I It Am, the light and the face that is all blessed love. I It Am, the Trinity. I It Am, the unity. I It Am, the high sovereign goodness of all manner of things. I It Am, that maketh thee to long. I It Am, the endless fulfilling of all true desires.*[8]

1. *Quoted in Robert W. Funk,* Parables and Presence, *Fortress Press, Philadelphia, 1982,* p. 130.
2. *Ruth 1:16-17*

33

3. *Edward Schillebeeckx*, Christ: The Christian Experience in the Modern World, *SCM, London, 1980, p. 35.*
4. *Gwen Harwood, 'I am the Captain of my Soul' from* Selected Poems, *Angus and Robertson, Sydney, 1990, p. 21.*
5. *Anne Elder, 'Crazy Woman' from* Crazy Woman and Other Poems, *Angus and Robertson, Sydney, 1976, p. 5.*
6. *ibid, p. 6.*
7. *Matthew 25:31–46.*
8. *Julian of Norwich,* A Showing of God's Love, *ed. Anne Maria Reynolds, Sheed and Ward, London, 1974, p. 38.*

Calling God Names

Janet Gaden

November 1988

ear God,

Some of our friends have been discussing what we feel able to call you.[1] I find this a difficult question, and I'd like to work out what answers I, myself, can live with. Since what I call you affects our relationship, and, therefore, affects you, I want to do my thinking about it in company with you; hence this letter.

See how many problems I get into simply in getting started! The first is one about language. When I speak to you about my conversation with my friends it sounds as if you were not present in it. This is a problem for all language addressed to you; how can we say anything to you or call you anything without making you seem distant by this very act of recalling your presence?

The second problem, on a personal level, is an issue of spirituality. I notice how quickly I move from 'we' to 'I'. While I believe you are most to be found in relationships, I am formed by a tradition that turns inward to be with you. So I set out eagerly to explore my relationship with you, ready to forget that what I call you affects my relating to my friends. As you are in us and we in you, we relate to each other in the light of our perceptions of you.

I will need to return to each of these issues. I raise them now to confess who I am and where I start from: a 'Western' (Australian) white woman still held in the attitudes of patriarchal Church tradition and capitalist spirituality, who though struggling against them, has grasped the hope of a freer and more loving relating in you.

Well, speaking for myself as I am, what can I call you?

If I call you 'Father', as the institutional Church almost always does, I am saying that you are half-way responsible for making me, that you are half the source of my life. But I don't want to underestimate you.

If I call you 'Father', I can't help bringing to mind my father, who, good man as he was, made his mistakes with me, as a result of which I have internalised a self-judging habit, a fear of acting with power, which I now see as precisely *ungodly*.

I am speaking personally, but I know I am in plenty of company. "Our maker and our judge", we say; "Father, forgive us": how quickly the father image turns on us to stress not relationship but our alienation and sense of sin. My father was as much a victim of this theology as I am: he felt called upon to act out the judge role against his own gentle nature.

If I call you 'Father', I will experience you as my culture has experienced fathers. For generations fathers have demonstrated their loving providence by being out at work. I do not want an absent God whose activity is elsewhere, whose providence is remote. I want to be around where you are working, to copy you and learn to work with you. I need to learn that what you do, I can do also, and not only when I grow up, but now. In farming and cottage-industry cultures, 'Father' may convey this experience, as it seems to have done for Jesus (John 5:19–20), but not where I live, not any more.

"When I grow up": there's another problem with calling you 'Father'. It says I am permanently and essentially immature. Like so many of my sisters, I am working hard against social pressures on women to remain immature. I don't need theological pressures as well. We talk about being 'children of God', but I understand that you'd rather have colleagues and friends, people who have grown, as you wish, "to the fullness of stature of Christ".

If I *as a woman* call you 'Father', I am saying that I can never, even "when I grow up", be like you; you are absolutely other. But you are the *incarnate* God, both other and one with all humanity. Nothing can separate me from you, but this name comes close to doing that, as it has been used and overused in our tradition.

The consequences of what I have been putting in personal terms are bad enough in the cramping of individual lives; they are still more damaging for your world. From Old Testament times you have also been seen as monarch, an absolute power, and this image has tangled with that of father, infecting it, so that you have been imaged as a distant, judging, overwhelmingly powerful and fear-producing father, one who protects us by destroying "our enemies".

Jesus' effort to reclaim your tenderness and close relating

37

by calling you 'Abba' never caught on. Still today the idolatrous image of you as God the Father Almighty, enthroned on a judgment seat located outside this world, sanctions the use of power against whoever or whatever we judge to be "our enemies". As our destructive power increases, it becomes clearer that this image is life-threatening, not just to individuals or even peoples, but to the planet.[2]

So despite the ancient tradition of the Church by which you have been called 'Father' most of the time—despite the example of Jesus "your Son"—I find I cannot call you 'Father'. Integrity forbids it—both my self-understanding and my desire to speak as truthfully as I can of you. But many women and some men have already said as much.

If I call you 'Mother', many of these problems remain; you are still only half creator, I am still permanently infantile. Human mothers have our own ways of cramping our children's growth, and our own load of negative associations.[3] We too may be out at work.

But if I as a woman call you 'Mother', I do experience a shock of recognition, of myself as like you, of you akin to me, which catches my cooler reason by surprise. In private prayer I sometimes change the psalmists' he into she (speaking of you as well as of myself) and bask in the increase of intimacy this brings to the text for me.

As I reflect on this experience, I realise how tightly my image of you is related to my estimate of myself. If I were unable to speak of you in feminine forms, I would be unable to see myself as godly, and my femaleness as good.[4] I don't mean the second is simply a consequence of the first; they grow together. As I became aware of the alienating effect on me of all-male imagery of you, I learned to see other women, and indeed myself, as embodying you, and this in turn rounded out my sense of you. So I understand the desire of some women and men to correct the old imbalance of the father image by emphasising the mother in you, though this is not what I want to call you.

Once I gave a paper exploring the possibilities of mother images for your action in the Eucharist.[5] Woman who are not literally mothers responded with more anger than I have ever

heard expressed about "God the Father". Why? As I understand
them, at first they believed themselves included in a new way
by the feminine images, then were the more disappointed to
find it not so. Also they rejected what they saw as a stereotypic
reduction of women to motherhood, and as yet one more
example of the Church's failure to recognise single and childless
people by the insistent linking of godliness and parenthood.
I could reply that these objections are unduly literal-minded
about images, parallel to the conclusion that if you may be
spoken of as 'Father' you must be a male. Nevertheless, I want
to take seriously these women's responses, and they make me
cautious about calling you 'Mother'.

I worry, too, that the urge to call you 'Mother', frequently
arises from and feeds a romantic feminism that looks to 'the
feminine' as all nurturing, creative, intuitive, receptive goodness—the comfortable virtues—over against the more rugged
'masculine'. But you are not a particularly soft or comfortable
God; nor are women, made in your image, that way either.
As Janet Morley has well pointed out,[6] it is actually dangerous
for women to ascribe femininity to you, because then, as we
wrestle with your toughness, strangeness and wrath, we must
confront these uncomfortable strengths in ourselves and in
our sisters. She is in favour of danger, as I am; it is the air
we breathe in approaching you.

On the whole I agree with Mary Daly that a sex-change
is not going to help you, or to solve our problems in relating
to you.[7] Calling you 'Mother' may be a useful teaching and
self-teaching strategy along the way, but in the end 'Mother'
is no better a name for you than 'Father'. What we need is
a freer, more adult and mutual way of relating to you.

What did you think of Sallie McFague's book about you,
Models of God? She says many things I'd like to have said, the
basic one being that we need to call you by many names if
we are to begin to explore the richness of your relating. I like
some of her work on calling you 'Mother'—though it's a bit
romantic—but I find the models of 'Lover' and 'Friend' more
promising, because these are mutual relations: if you are my
lover and friend, I am your lover and friend.

I say this last with a passion. I need it to be so. I yearn

for a relation of mutuality with you, the relation of lover and friend. In terms of my theological upbringing, to entertain such a thought is nonsense, blasphemous nonsense. In that tradition, you are Above, you are the self-sufficient Almighty. I am all finitude and fallenness; nothing of me is found in you. Yet I do not only yearn for mutuality; to some extent I experience it.

I said before that I go inward to find you, but it seems to me now that in fact I image you not within but beside me. When I pray you are sitting at my side. We walk shoulder to shoulder together. I do not experience you as the controller of my life but as fellow-sufferer in it, not holding me in your great big palm but in your friend-sized arms, as you weep or rejoice with me. I experience you as sister-companion in the struggle for becoming, that is to say, as co-creatrix. (There you are—the Trinity in terms of mutual relating!) Our relationship is not entirely mutual and equal, but I believe you are calling me that way.

As healer or spiritual director, my work is to move with the other person into a place where the asymmetrical relationship can be outgrown, and we can part on equal terms or remain as friends. So it is in your work with me. If a relationship is unequal in power and intends to stay that way, it is a kind of abuse, debasing both parties. I have met people who are abused by their image of you, but you are not an abusive God. You are the kenotic God, emptying yourself, pouring out your loving power to empower me and all your creation.

To call you 'Lover' and 'Friend' has the further advantage that these images are personal without imputing to you a gender which would limit you or separate you from any of us. But in naming these positives I raise more problems. You do not have gender,[8] but we have sexuality, which is basic to all our loving and relating, both to other people and to you. I cannot conceive that your love for me is less ardent and entire than mine for you. So while I say that you do not have gender, that our gendered images for you are misleading in that respect, I would not like you to think I want to keep sexuality out of talking about you, or to you.

40

When I say you are love, I mean you are passion; that you throw yourself into relationship with us, and into embodiment (incarnation) in this world, into joy and suffering and danger, out of a desire which, in us, is sexual at depth, however it is expressed. So we need ways of relating to you and thinking of you which make room for passion without making you in our image.

We seem to need human images for you. The only other kind of relating we know that is at all comparable, and gives us terms for trying to talk of our experience of you, is our relating to other people. But human images are not enough. You are more than human, and relate to more than humanity. How can I, if at all, get beyond my human-centred view of you and your creation? My human language and experience tend to cut you down to human size even when I try to speak of your transcendence.

I can, of course, include among your names many non-human images which I fill, as poets do, with an intensity that is personal while transcending human reference: My Rock, My Sun, Breath of All Living, Water of Life, Mighty Wind, Fire. I need to do this and work on it, because otherwise I assume that it is in humanity alone that you are incarnate, forgetting that the whole created order is "God's Body".[9]

My effort to stretch my picture of you is always an effort to make further connections. That's what you are really, isn't it: the Great Connector! But that sounds mechanical, which won't do: you are the Great Relater. And yet (here's the intriguing part), are you Relater or are you Relation itself? "In the beginning is the relation", says Carter Heyward often,[10] which sounds right to me, and I continue, as she may well mean me to—though I don't think she says it—"and relation is with God, and relation is God". So you are both relater and relationship itself. An image which puts this question about you very excitingly comes from a poem of D.H. Lawrence:

Water is H$_2$O, hydrogen two parts, oxygen one,
but there is also a third thing that makes it water
and nobody knows what that is.[11]

Now there is and there isn't a third thing.

41

The newness in water is the overcoming of an old dualism. As we struggle to free human thinking from the masculine/feminine dualism, where it is inappropriate, we need also to stop talking about us and you as if we were opposites forever distinct. I need to step aside from the rhetoric about you as the remote Almighty and me "a very worm and no man [even!]", I need to listen instead to how I am made in the spitting image of you; look to you alive in Jesus the human one (just as I am human); and attend to my baptism and all the sacramental life of the Church in which I participate, the whole point of which is to enflesh my identification with you.

Identification with you; that is what is most important to me, most difficult to think of and to feel, but still more difficult to speak of. How can I speak of you without distancing myself from you? I am speaking to you now, rather than about you, as more formal theologians do, because I refuse to talk as if you were somewhere else, to talk behind your back, at a safe distance, as it were. That is, I don't want to talk 'objectively', academically about you.

I feel a little less impertinent this way, if only because to address you directly feels more loving and more risky. I risk sounding naive, not clever; the 'wise fool' may be just a fool. It is the same risk you took in Jesus, in fact it is you who are taking the risk in me.

But does the act of talking to you in itself set up a dualism, make us too distinct, keep us apart? It seems so. Yet sometimes, when I talk or write to a friend, although I am truly addressing her, I am speaking so personally and riskily that what I say is news to me also. So I am simultaneously speaking to my friend and to myself, not in two acts but one: so we *commune*, we are 'one together'.

That can happen between you and me in prayer. At those times I don't call you anything. Sometimes we talk in tongues, love-talk without conscious content; this is the closest I've come to experiencing speech which does not divide speaker from spoken to. Some of my discomfort in writing all this comes from my experience in my prayer—that if I am talking to you a lot I am evading you, trying to keep you apart from me; the 'safe distance' illusion again. At my best and bravest, I prefer just to *be with you*, in silence. In silence we reach a deeper relation than one to one, like lovers who 'are one'.

Yet as soon as I become aware of this state, I reflect, I verbalise, and this act separates us. Can I be one with you only so long as I don't know it, or say so, or talk about it? But Jesus did all of these. "The Father and I are one", he said (John 10:30), and I believe him, although his grammar makes you two. And the grammar is right, after all. Although Jesus incarnated you as perfectly as a human can, because you are more than human even he could not embody all of you: so, "The Father is greater than I" (John 14:28).

This is one truth I hear in the language of Trinity. I also hear that even in your own oneness there is distinction. Of course, the Trinity is as much a human construct as any other imagery by which we talk about you. So what I'm hearing in it is a human work of reconciliation for the impasse I thought I was in. The Trinity, which is the best unity we can imagine, is unity in relationship, and as such it embraces and celebrates distinctions. To be one with you is not necessarily to merge mystically with you. I can be my conscious individual self and still know myself as one with you.

How can I celebrate and share this closeness with you, extending it into my dealings with other people? Not by speaking of you so much as by incarnating you; by 'godding', as is said,[12] in the world.

I incarnate you? How I fear to claim this obvious truth, and hide from my own human power to do good, make justice, and mend your bruised creation. Yet I know that, as I am a part of your created world—your body—you act and are present only in and through me and other creatures. I fear my power to incarnate you because of the responsibility that goes with the power: if I can do this, I must. And the cost is great. This we see most clearly in Jesus, as in him we see most clearly what incarnation means: to be truly human *is* to be truly God. To love you is to embody you, to 'god', do good, make justice, make right relation.

I can't do that on my own, sitting at prayer, though to keep at it I do need to sit at prayer with you. It is not really *I* who relate to you, or embody you, but *we*, people together.

43

I spoke of being at one with you in certain kinds of prayer; the other context where I experience that oneness is when I am single-mindedly, absorbedly 'godding', doing your work with other people.

People 'god' where two or three are gathered together, consciously or unconsciously in the name of right relation. Communities can 'god'. The wider, seemingly impersonal structures a society builds for its life can 'god', though they generally don't. They 'god' as they act for justice, for right relation. "In the beginning is the relation"—and relation is with God and relation is God.

If you are relation, and I think you are, do you then disappear as an entity in yourself? I think you do. I suppose this is what is meant by that abstract talk of you as Be–ing itself; Being, not a being. Language conceals the implication of this insight; 'Being', like 'God', still sounds like something or someone. It sounds like a noun, not a verb. "God the Verb", Mary Daly paradoxically calls you.[13] The phrase points up the difficulty of thinking of you as acting rather than actor.

If you are not an entity, then it makes no sense to address you at all. And yet I do address you, as people always have. Indeed, I talk to you increasingly as I get surer that this makes no sense.

Now I wonder if this means I'm in an awkward stage of growth, or if it's a dissociation in myself that I need to attend to, or if my prayer is telling my theology something important. But this isn't just my individual situation. Although it makes no sense, it reflects how you are.[14] My puzzlement is an uncomfortable legacy from my Western theological fathers, who have sought you in thought and word. Their theology of the word is now being challenged, extended and made more complete by women and non-Western theologians, who seek you first in deed, in experience and shared action, and for whom verbal reflection is but one part of that. I am being stretched between the two.

I'm embarrassed by the place I've come to, rejecting traditional ways of naming you, having no better solution to offer, wanting to talk to you, wanting more to relate to you immediately without speech, feeling that all this is somehow address-

ing the wrong question. But no, I have come to a good place—
of transformation and an evergrowing sense of your mystery—
by which, my love, I'm brought to silence.

Yours,

Janet

1. *A list of the printed contributions to this conversation would be enormous, and has lengthened since this letter was written. A friend has sent me Carter Heyward's* Touching Our Strength: the Erotic as Power and the Love of God, *Harper & Row, New York, 1989, which I would have loved to take into account.*
2. *Sallie McFague,* Models of God: Theology for an Ecological Nuclear Age, *SCM, London, 1987.*
3. *For example, Dorothy Dinnerstein,* The Mermaid and the Minotaur: Sexual Arrangements and the Human Malaise, *Harper & Row, New York, 1976.*
4. *On this point see Kathleen Fischer,* Women at the Well: Feminist Perspectives on Spiritual Direction, *SPCK, London, 1989, especially chapter 3, 'Women Experiencing and Naming God'.*
5. *Janet and John Gaden, 'Eucharistic Community' in* Coming Together: Proceedings of the Second National Conference of MOW Australia, *ed. Janet Gaden, Adelaide, 1986.*
6. *Janet Morley, 'Liturgy and Danger' in* Mirror to the Church, *ed. Monica Furlong, SPCK, London, 1988, especially pp. 32–3.*
7. *Mary Daly,* Beyond God the Father, *Women's Press, London, 1985.*
8. *Here and throughout I use the word 'gender' in the grammatical and general sense, not the sociological: that is, of words, having a masculine/feminine form or sense; of beings, having one or other sex. So I call 'Father' and 'Mother' gendered images, while 'Lover' and 'Friend' are not gender-specific, although they involve sexuality.*
9. *Grace Jantzen,* God's World, God's Body, *Westminster Press, Louisville, 1984.*
10. *Carter Heyward,* The Redemption of God: A Theology of Mutual Relation, *University Press of America, Washington, DC, 1982, p. 1, etc. She is quoting Martin Buber.*
11. *D.H. Lawrence,* Birds, Beasts and the Third Thing, *Julia MacRae Books, London, 1982.*
12. *For example, Carter Heyward,* Redemption of God; *Virginia Mollenkott,* Godding: Human Responsibility and the Bible, *Crossroad, New York, 1987.*
13. *Daly, p. 33.*
14. *Maggie Ross,* Pillars of Flame: Power, Priesthood and Spiritual Maturity, *SCM, London, 1988, p. x, notes "the resemblance between Ephrem's strand of Semitic Christianity that insists that it is blasphemous to posit God—God can be engaged but not posited—and our postmodernist gropings toward what is unsayable". She points out the presence of Ephrem's insight "in the West from Irenaeus through Augustine, to be found also in Luther, Tillich, Buber and Heschel".*

Adding My Piece

John R. Gaden

January 1989

ear Janet,

You kindly showed me your letter to God and I felt moved to respond. It's good to be in the company of those who work out their theology in addressing God!

As you know, I have recently taught a course on the history of spirituality. What struck me as I read your letter was the way your concerns echoed much in the apophatic or negative tradition of prayer. Within the Christian community there have always been those who came to God beyond words, beyond names. The name above every other name (cf. Ephesians 1:21) is in a sense nameless. The name given in the burning bush is a no-name (Exodus 3:13f).

This is the position of the classic sixth century treatise by Pseudo-Dionysius on *The Divine Names*, reflected also in the writings of Meister Eckhart. From the fourteenth century English school, *The Cloud of Unknowing* states that God is not known by words but love, not in the mind but in the heart.[1] Thinking and names, only create a barrier between ourselves and God.

However, most writers in this tradition of prayer fail on two critical points: they make little or nothing of the Incarnation or of relationships. Both of these are of central importance for you, and I hope you can go further in holding embodied relationships together with the way of silence. They seem fundamentally so opposed, but the God beyond all naming is named Abba, Jesus, Spirit, Love, and is known in acts of mercy, grace and justice.

John 14:6–17 clarifies this for me and also interprets the Johannine text to which you refer, "The Father and I are one" (John 10:30). Philip says, "Lord, show us the Father [i.e., God] and then we shall be satisfied" (John 14:8), yet at the beginning of the Gospel it is asserted, "No one has ever seen God" (1:18). Jesus responds by declaring that to see him is to see the Father, because Father and Son mutually indwell each other. Jesus' words and works are those of the Father operating in him. God is seen in the relating of Father and Son which becomes visible in what Jesus says and does. As you say, God is both the relating ("The Father and I are one") and the fruit of the relating ("It is the Father, living in me, who is doing his works", John 14:10).

But it doesn't stop there. Those who believe in Jesus experience the same relating. They do the works that make God visible through the Spirit that dwells in them, and that work is above all love one for another. So when the Johannine school draws the conclusion that "God is love" (1 John 4:8), the word 'love' means acts of love, loving, relating. To love another is to see God, indeed, to be God. I and God are one: *ubi caritas, deus ibi est*. As in the mystical tradition, the line between God and us becomes blurred: we are engaged, as you say, in 'godding'. But in the opening up of some new possibility for human beings, in an unexpected deed of kindness, in our love for each other, there is something beyond words, where silence is the ultimate response. Yet we do say something, or I do, that speaks not only of the other but of what is happening between us—"How good to be here", as well as, "You are amazing". Words form part of the relating.

I take the Father-Son language in John's Gospel to refer to the relating which is God. Because this relating involves much more than you and me, our friends, and the society in which we live, but includes the whole history and life of the universe, I acknowledge God as transcendent. God is not just the sum of all my activities. "The Father is greater than I" (John 14:28). Similarly, God is more than Father, because God could not be unrelated. God is Father, Son and Spirit, relating within the mystery of God and at the same time to the world. It is the relating which is important, not the name we give God. We would perhaps find other names for these relationships in God, as the Cappadocians and Augustine did.

But people have trouble with triangular relationships and relating closely to (or in) a trinity is even harder. That is exactly the problem, as you yourself are aware. The personal language of prayer derives from our experience of one-to-one relating. Monogamy, monotheism, and the alone with the alone are all connected. Very few prayers are addressed directly to the Trinity. We invoke God, Lord, Father, Jesus, Christ, Spirit, Wisdom, Mother, Friend, Lover, and imagine *one* person not three.

Liturgically and devotionally people seem to be Arian or Unitarian, unable to take on board the full Trinitarian bit.

I don't handle this very well myself, either. I am conscious enough of quite deliberately moving from image to image, from Person to Person, depending on my mood or need. In that way I try to overcome fixation on any one image and an unbalanced, un-Trinitarian experience of God. At times I am also aware of being with Jesus and all my sisters and brothers who are making up the Christ, in the gracious presence of the Source of all being, and all this happening through the Holy Spirit in me. When I want to put a face on this presence, I see Jesus. When I am asked to identify this God, I say 'living, energizing Spirit'. For such a God, 'Father' is altogether inadequate, for all the reasons you mentioned, and more besides.

One issue, in particular, that this raises for me is the responses in the Australian Values Survey on the kind of God people believe in.[2] Given a choice between a personal God and an impersonal force—itself a false dichotomy in naming God—believers came down almost equally between the two. As we know from the *Honest to God* debate of twenty-five years ago, many Christians find the idea of God as a person (or even an entity) quite unacceptable, as do you and I, but that is what is conjured up by the term 'a personal God'. I suspect that many people like myself believe in a power of life or source of being, experienced in the quiet of the bush, a luxuriant spring, the vastness of desert and night sky, a refreshing creek, the endless waves, intimate relationships, working together, the flow of things, social movements, etc.

For such an experience, Spirit is a better word than Father or Mother. Part of our evangelistic task is to persuade such believers that this Spirit is found most humanly in Jesus, and is available to energise people in those communities who gather to keep alive the vision of relating which is embodied in Jesus.

Very early on in the current Australian debate about the ordination of women, you will remember that I wrote a paper on the androgynous God.[3] I would wish now to distance myself somewhat from that notion if it suggests that God is both male and female. You and I are agreed that this is inadequate because it still reduces God to a person. Now I would prefer to say that both male and female experiences provide imagery that is appropriately used of God, some of it gender-based and some of it inclusive, but to restrict one's language for God to this range belittles God. There is much more to say about God—the work that you and others are doing on relating and 'godding', my concern for the experience of God as living Spirit.

Of course, just as you want to say that the relating is shared by both women and men, so do I affirm that the living, energising Spirit finds human embodiment in women equally with men. The Christ is made up of both sexes alike. But there is more to reality and life than male and female and in that knowledge I hope we will continue to encourage each other to keep on moving in.

With love, in Relating,

John

1. The Cloud of Unknowing, 6.
2. *See Peter Marshall, 'The Domestication of the Church',* St Mark's Review, *18, Sept. 1984, pp. 3–12.*
3. *John R. Gaden,* Women and the Ministry, *Christ Church Press, Brunswick, 1976, pp. 5–13.*

Postscript
Janet Gaden

ear John,   June 1991
      As I retyped your reply for publication I was
thinking, "What a pity it's not fair to reply to
this now", now that you are dead and can't reply
again, but at last I see that this needn't stop me. In any conversation, someone has the last word. In what I want to say
to you, I want to talk about silence, and your silence now
will be part of that. I will also be saying some more about
a point that I made but did not develop in my letter to God:
how I image God and relate with God directly affects my
relating to other people. Indeed, the connection is closer yet;
how I image and relate with God is part of my relating and
part of who I am. It is integral to my relating with you.

      You are right to put my letter to God in the apophatic
line of spirituality, yet in my life I'm more of a mixture. I have
remarked to you before how odd it feels to me to work with
other people through story and verbal meditation, image and
word, and then go home to wordless, imageless prayer. I
remember I worried that one of these styles must be phony—
but now I think of them more as a rich roundedness, a wholeness to value. I remember you replied that, conversely, you
set out to teach the prayer of quiet, prizing it highly, yet had
trouble with it yourself. I don't think we actually thought we
had to be apophatic or cataphatic purists; we knew better in
dealing with other people, saying, "However you pray best,
pray like that". I suppose we were exploring the difference
in the way each of us was balanced, with me closer to the
wordless pole than you were. Thus, my mode of quietening
is the feel of the breath, yours that verbal mantra, the Jesus
prayer. This balance is both a matter of personal style and
the variety of God's self-revelation.

      I'm interested that you say "embodied relationships and
the way of silence... seem fundamentally so opposed"; to me
they seem fundamentally joined. I remember some marriage
workshop where we had to talk to each other at depth, to
order—and how we resented it. You felt as if we were being
told to make love to order. Well, we were; talking at real, costly
depth is a kind of lovemaking, as it is one kind of prayer.

I felt we were being told to fake it; real bodily lovemaking has little need for talk, and this command violated a silence better than speech.

Anyway, we had to say what we didn't do well—not a constructive task, I thought, but despite my resistances I found myself saying that what I failed to do was to *tell* you that I love you. "I do it", I said, "and show it, but I don't say it". Then and since, I've understood this as failure and felt guilty even. So I am smitten by your saying, "Yet we do say something, or I do,... 'You are amazing'". Yet I am sure you knew yourself loved as much as I did. Only now do I connect our different love behaviour with our prayer experience. Only now do I really pay attention to the phrase: "With my body I thee worship", and hear in it an affirmation of embodied relationship in the way of silence.

I remember too the Easter joy of running to meet the hearse bringing your body home from Sydney, after the days of your utter absence and hiddenness: "They have taken away my Lord and I know not where they have laid him". I remember the days and nights when you lay in the college chapel and I sat beside you, hour after hour in silence. Silence and touch. You were amazing. This was no empty shell; this was your whole self amazingly concentrated and focussed in your silence, which was like the silence of God.

Why do we so often think of the silence of God as absence? There is a silence which is absence, hostility or indifference, and there is a silence which is intense engagement. How we interpret God's silence also depends on how we image God, and ourselves before God; whether the God we live with is the monarch or the companion-God.

The monarch-God's approaches are commands or directions, making known his will for the believer. The believer's address to God will be petitions that God will act or speak, and the answer to prayer will be God's action or word (intervention: act and word are practically identical). I have listened to believers in this God as they speak of the pain of God's silence. As I understand them, they interpret this in a combination of three main ways. First, as a sign that God the monarch was not listening or was too busy; that they themselves are not worth God's attention. Or, secondly, God has refused their petition, either because they asked the wrong thing or because at worst God does not wish their wellbeing. Either way, God's silence shows that God is indifferent to them, or displeased or angry or hostile or malevolent. It's a sign of a breakdown in relationship between them and God, so it causes distress and fear.

Such people can either blame themselves, finding their own unworthiness or guilt central in the experience, or they can blame and reject God. As an extreme of this, thirdly, they can decide that such a hostile monarch-God makes no sense at all, and if this is the only God they know of, they may conclude that God does not exist. With this understanding of God, silence is and leads to rejection, estrangement and absence.

The silence of the companion-God, on the other hand, is a mode of being present. The silent Companion waits, gives me space to say more, to change and to grow. The silent Companion is listening to me, as to all creation—listening and letting be. The Companion's silence is a self-restraint exercised in my interest, taking care not to intervene and satisfy me too soon, which might cut short my maturing. If the companion-God 'does not answer' my prayer, I do not need to take this for a refusal which sends me back to square one. It is an invitation to me to come in closer, desire more boldly, ask for more.

I welcome the silence of the companion-God whom I experience. Silence is what I expect, because I experience the way of silence as fundamentally related to close, embodied relationship. This silent Companion is silent *because* so close, standing with me, feeling what I feel, and there is nothing to say. The Companion holds me, weeping or dancing, and there is no need to speak. Or we are working and walking side by side and the effort is more like touch than speech.

I do not know whether I experience God in this way because this is how I have related with you, or whether it's the other way round. Similarly, do I place such importance on silence and listening in personal and pastoral relating because I experience God's silence as 'wholemaking', or is it the other way round? The questions are misguided, and the answer is: neither.

How I relate to (name or image) God is part of who I am and how I relate.

What has it done to my imaging of God and to my relating that now I hold so intensely that time with you in your death as my most powerful experience of the presence of God?

One of our sons said of you in those days, "I wish we could keep him like that. I am learning contemplation from him now". It was true for all of us. Dead, you led me further in than I have ever been to the silent mystery that so attracts and terrifies me. At your funeral we sang (not my choice; resurrection talk grated on me unbearably for a long time, and is still very difficult):

Jesus lives, thy terrors now
Can no more, O death, appal us,

and it was true; death's terrors could no more appal us. Not because Jesus lives, however, but because you died. Because the worst possible had already happened. Above all, because in the long days and nights of becoming familiar with your deadness, watching you, touching you, anointing you, making eucharist with you, picnicking beside you in the sanctuary, talking to you and falling silent, we had been able to make peace with the appalling fact, and with letting you go.

Yet it remains appalling. I am less afraid of death now than before, but no less afraid of coming before God in silence. What I have written to God and to you about the Companion-God is incomplete without acknowledgment of the fear of God, which is not the monopoly of the Monarch. Why do I resist with fear the experience I most treasure—that of entering in silence the silent presence of the loving God who invites me?

One obvious guess is that the silence and stillness of contemplative prayer so closely mimics death that my basic human animal instinct of self-preservation rises up to avoid it. My mix of fear and attraction about prayer does run parallel to my feelings about my own death, since you died. But there's more to it than that. I don't just fear silence because it is deathlike and appalling, I fear it because it is ecstatic and wonderful, because it is the *best* that can happen.[1] Now why is this so?

Fear of ecstatic union with God in silence is about fear

57

of *ecstasy*, of being beside myself, *of losing control*. It is as much like the fear of letting go in sexual lovemaking as it is like the fear of death. I reflect on the expression I learned in Elizabethan love poetry: 'to come' is 'to die'. To come into the presence of God is to die by abandoning all self-consciousness and control.

Again and again I hear Christian mysticism defended as not being like 'Eastern' types because its experience of divine union does not involve the dissolution of the self. I'm not so sure. Not as a permanent and literal ontological fact, I agree; we return to ourselves and persist. But as experience, I think that is what it is about. Indeed, this is one part of what is meant by the Pauline paradox about 'dying we live', or Jesus' words, 'Whoever loses life for my sake will gain it', and is continuous with ways of living out those words in personal-political struggle.

We Christians pay lipservice to these paradoxes, to the life-giving power of dying, of self-emptying, of surrender to the love of God. Yet Christian terror of these things has been painfully clear to both of us. What can still appal me is the depth of the denial of death, by trivialisation, by cheap resurrection cheer as well as by simple avoidance, in the responses of church people to my grief for you. I have suffered and seen you suffer from the terror of good church people at the thought of real live sexuality, especially of life-giving ecstacy in sexual experience that is different from their own and beyond their control—whether of women as such or of open lesbians and gay men. You broke taboo by being too little afraid; you were a sign of hope and danger, and you paid.

I remember now Carter Heyward's powerful words about this fear:

> I am convinced that to the extent that we are afraid of our sexual being, we're afraid of God, because what is God if not the wellspring of our creativity, our relationality, our ecstasy, our capacity to touch and be touched at the core of our being?[2]

Yet we all say: 'the Word was made flesh'. In the infant Jesus we see the whole power of God present in a speechless child who can only suck and stroke and cuddle and sleep.

So we affirm that the wisdom of God is fully present in bodily loving, in silent touch. But:

A Word made Flesh is seldom
And tremblingly partook
Nor then perhaps reported
But have I not mistook
Each one of us has tasted
With ecstasies of stealth
The very food debated
To our specific strength—[3]

'Ecstasies of stealth'—what a phrase, both for a passionate approach to the mystery and/or a double-hearted denial of the power that draws us!

A Word that breathes distinctly
Has not the power to die
Cohesive as the Spirit
It may expire...[4]

John, I like to think, as Karl Rahner suggests somewhere, that when we expire, our final bodily consenting to let go and lose control and 'give up the ghost' (whether our will consents or not) is the consent to union with God by which we are brought out from our resistances and fully into God's embrace.

But for now I find myself in a bind with God. If my God were the Monarch who is all power, I would not be in this bind, but as I grow in love for the Lover-Companion God, the bind pulls tighter. I yearn for union with God. But the God I desire is the self-emptying, self-limiting, silent and silenced God I see on the Cross in Jesus and in the coffin in you. I fear this self-emptying as much as I desire it. Nor can I escape this bind; Lord, where would I go?

So I embrace this cross of desire and fear. I try, as you did, John, to embrace vulnerability as a way of life. Your autopsy showed you were in perfect health, you had a good strong heart in good condition. But it broke. You died brokenhearted from carrying other people's terror, destructively expressed. The trick is, you used to say, to absorb: that is, to be utterly vulnerable. The buck stops at the Cross.

That was the burden of my first ever sermon at the Women's

World Day of Prayer in 1965! It's a pattern running through our life and work together. At the very time you were dying, I was intensely reading the story of 'Lissener', who absorbs the destructiveness that wants to rub out the world and listens things back into life.[5] He can listen all the time because he is blind and defenceless, and he is killed in the end, but his voice is strong with joy.

As I go on living and working in the way of vulnerability, I have been repairing your Cowley cloak, which you've had since we were newly married. You wore it in cold weather to go over to the chapel to say the offices. It's riddled with moth holes, but it feels wonderful to wear, like a blanket that folds me but doesn't hobble me. Besides, to me it feels like being wrapped in you. So I badly want to wear it too, as a prayer shawl and the mantle of Elijah.

But here's the good bit. It is *so* moth-eaten, really. There would be so many darns it would look awful, however neatly done. So I have been crocheting woollen flowers to decorate the moth-holes. Lots of maroon roses and purple daisies and deep blue borage flowers and dark green leaves. But there are so many holes! When I hold it open against the light it looks like the starry sky. Indeed, I think working on it is making more come. So I hear my mother and all sensible people including myself saying that it's a terrible waste of time and work. Why don't I put this energy into a new bit of cloth that will last?

The thing is, though, this cloak is a celebration of 'holeyness' and flaws. The more I work it, the more I wear it, the more tattered it will get and the more flowers will grow there to proclaim vulnerability as the power in healing and the aim of prayer, and the connection that is blessing will be made through the holes. Amen.

With love,

Janet

1. *A chapter, "Resistance to union: a virulent strain" from William Barry,* Paying attention to God, *started me thinking like this.*
2. *The Mudflower Collective:* God's Fierce Whimsy, *The Pilgrim Press, New York, 1985.*
3. *Emily Dickinson, 'A Word made Flesh', from* The Complete Poems of Emily Dickinson, *edited by Thomas H. Johnson, Faber & Faber, London, 1970, pp 675, 676.*
4. *ibid.*
5. *Russell Hoban,* Riddley Walker, *quoted as the epigraph to Maggie Ross,* Pillars of Flame, *SCM Press, London, 1988.*

Women:
Less than Free in
Christ's Church
Rt Rev. John S. Spong

rganised religious systems serve many human functions that are not always conscious. A major function has been to define life and to exert the necessary control to see that all people adhere to that definition. One can thus study the religions of the world and through that means begin to understand the culturally-assumed definitions of human sexuality and sexual roles allowed and blessed in the areas where the various religions are dominant.

To look briefly at the sexual implications of the other religions of the world helps us to focus on the Western attitude toward women. In this process, even assumptions we thought were innate and natural prove to be relative, and a new objectivity arises about how our own religious tradition has defined each of our roles and stamped us with our own sexual understandings.

The first observation that such a study reveals is that the religious systems which developed in the Western world are more intensely anti-female than are those of any other religious tradition. Judaism, Christianity, and Islam have an exclusively masculine understanding of God. No female divine figure is in the pantheon of any of these three religious systems. Hera, the wife of Zeus, or Juno, the wife of Jupiter, did not find a new incarnation in Western religious symbols.

In India, by contrast, the divine trinity, if we might use that phrase, is Shiva, the Father God; Shakti, his wife; and Vishnu, another male. Shiva and Shakti were often portrayed in Oriental art in passionate embraces so sensuous that modern-day puritans would be shocked.[1] There was no apparent need to deny or suppress the physical pleasures in Hinduism. Both the male and the female bodies were considered part of the human being, not separate from or over against the spirit. Fulfilment of the total human being, and not the suppression of the body and its physical appetites, was a dominating motif.

In Chinese philosophy the feminine principle is represented as an equal power in the dynamic tension of life which was pictorially expressed as the yin and the yang. The yin was feminine, representing the dark, mysterious, receptive, intuitive

64

quality of life. It was contemplative and restful. The yin was identified with the earth, which was in most ancient traditions assumed to be feminine and called Mother Earth.

The yang on the other hand was the masculine principle. It represented the light of rationality and intellect. Action-oriented, strong, and aggressive, the yang was identified with the sky, the heavens, the creative powers. From the sky, the realm of the yang, the rain, thought to be the divine semen, fell to impregnate Mother Earth, the realm of the yin, so that life could emerge. The active dynamism of the yang always confronted the quiet, still, sagelike quality of the yin.

Despite the sexual typecasting present in these Chinese symbols, there was, in fact, no overt sense of superiority and inferiority between the yin and the yang. Theirs was the tension of equals, and a sense of wholeness was created by their mutual inescapability. They were both caught in a dynamic cyclical relationship, and each possessed within itself a bit of the other. Nothing was purely yin or purely yang. Which is another way of saying that nothing was either purely feminine or purely masculine. The balance was perfect and the tension eternal.

I do not mean to suggest that the Eastern traditions escaped the misogyny that I submit was universal. Certainly the pattern of the wife walking three paces behind the husband, and the cruel binding of the female's feet, which served to create deeper dependency by curbing mobility, are sufficient examples. In Japan the word woman is even used to apply to a slow and stupid man. The Chinese character for woman is the word 'noisy' repeated three times.[2] The status of women in Eastern cultures does not appear to be enhanced by this theological inclusiveness. Nonetheless it is true that the Orient appears to have affirmed the value of feminine reality in its concept of God far more significantly than the West has ever done.

The sexual definitions in the Western tradition certainly reveal a vastly different and in many ways more hostile under-standing of women. The negativity toward women, so ancient in its origin, was not countered by a divine feminine figure, and it became powerfully operative. Women were assigned a status that was less than fully human. A prayer in the auth-orised Jewish Daily Prayer book said, "Blessed art thou, O Lord our God, King of the Universe, who hast not made me a woman."

In contradistinction to the dynamic sexual tension of the East, the religious rhetoric of the West assumed that men formed the legitimate body of the community and that women were allowed to participate only when they assimilated themselves into the male society. In *The Timaeus* Plato considered that "a man who led a good life might return to his native star; but if he did not, he might come back to earth as a woman."[3] Clearly, to be a woman was punishment. The power of a curse still accompanied the woman, even in the lofty phrases of the great thinker Plato.

Aristotle in *The Politics* casually asserted woman's natural inferiority during a discussion of animal life:

> *Again, the same holds true between man and the other animals: tame animals are superior in their nature to wild animals, yet for all the former it is advantageous to be ruled by man, since this gives them security. Also as between the sexes, the male is by nature superior and the female is inferior. The male is the ruler and the female is the subject.*[4]

Both *The Timaeus* and *The Politics* were frequently quoted by medieval scholars to justify the low status of women in later Western civilisation.

The Old Testament meshed with these Greek opinions to form an uncritical tradition. In the Ten Commandments women were listed among male possessions along with slaves, cattle and donkeys (Exodus 20:17). In the Garden of Eden story, sin entered the world through the weakness of a woman who was perceived as a secondary part of creation, lower than man while perhaps higher than animals, serving primarily as man's helpmate.

Into these prevailing attitudes the Christian Church was born and these attitudes were filtered through, modified by, and given a special new emphasis by that tradition.

In its earliest years, Christianity showed a remarkable openness to women. Jesus violated Jewish custom by talking with women and by allowing a woman of the street to wash and anoint his feet in a public place (Matthew 26:7ff). Clearly there were women in the band of disciples (Luke 23:27, Mark 15:40-1), though they do not appear to be numbered among the Twelve. All four Gospels written between AD 65 and 100 preserve the tradition that the Resurrection of our Lord was first announced to a group of women with Mary Magdalene being the central and consistent character in that drama (Matthew 28:1, Mark 16:1, Luke 24:10, John 20:1).[5] Luke tells us that "some women, including Mary the mother of Jesus" shared also in both the Ascension and Pentecost experiences of the early Church (Acts 1:14).

It seems clear that in the early period of Church history women held positions of leadership as prophets, teachers and evangelists. Despite ecclesiastical arguments to the contrary, the threefold ordered ministry of bishops, priests and deacons had not yet developed. The book of Acts tells us of Priscilla's vital role not only as a supporter of Paul (Acts 18:2, 18:18) but as the means through which Apollos, a male evangelist, "received more detailed instruction about the way of God" (Acts 18:26). Paul called Priscilla "my fellow worker in Christ Jesus" and wished the church "in her house" his greetings (Romans 16:3, 5). Paul commended to the Roman Christians a woman deacon named Phoebe, urging them to help her "for she herself has come to the help of many, including myself" (Romans 16:2). Romans was written in AD 56, more than thirty years before the Acts account of the choosing of the seven male deacons. Paul also singled out for greeting a woman named Mary "who worked so hard for you" (Romans 16:6). Cyril C. Richardson suggests that the Junias Paul salutes as an "apostle who was in Christ before me" (Romans 16:7) was, in fact, a woman, a point supported by the recent research of Professor B. Brooten.[6]

In 2 Timothy the author indicates that Timothy's faith was a gift to him from two generations of women—Lois, his grandmother, and Eunice, his mother. Professor Wayne Meeks suggests that the phrase "in Christ there is neither male nor female", which appears in Galatians 3:28, was originally a liturgical formula from an early Christian initiation rite.[7] If that theory proves to be accurate, it would represent a startling new consciousness that marked the early Christian movement.

These illustrations are not meant to suggest that the early Christian Church escaped or even modified too significantly the sexual attitudes of that day, but it does indicate that the power of the gospel was so pervasive that life 'in Christ' made all other barriers seem insignificant, at least for a time. However, even then and certainly continuing into our generation, the Christian Church has consistently represented God in totally masculine terms as Father, King, Lord, Master, Ruler and Judge. Paul, speaking out of the traditional orientation of his time, argued that since God is male, only men, not women, were created in God's image. Only man, therefore, "is the image of God and reflects God's glory", he argued, while "woman is the reflection of man's glory". He continued to press this point by asserting, "man did not come from woman; no, woman came from man; nor was man created for the sake of woman, but woman for the sake of man" (1 Corinthians 11:7-9).

Even this negative attitude, however, bore witness to the new consciousness, for one does not offer this kind of argument unless in answer to either a counterargument or a counter-practice. When Paul goes on to suggest that women must keep quiet in church, he reveals that he is in a polemic. Somewhere in the Church women were, in fact, not keeping quiet but rather were assuming a role and an authority which bent, if it did not break, the male-imposed female role model.

By the end of the first century, however, this new spirit of inclusiveness was diminished by a strong anti-woman mood that ultimately won the day. The pseudo-Pauline letters to Timothy and to the church at Ephesus were accepted by orthodox Christians as genuinely Pauline. Both exaggerated the anti-feminist element that was present but not quite so strident in the original Pauline corpus. "During instruction, a woman should be quiet and respectful", the letter to Timothy exhorted; "I give no permission for a woman to teach or to have authority over a man" (1 Timothy 2:11ff). This author went on with some vehemence to blame women for sin and to suggest that a woman's salvation would come through "child-bearing, provided she lives a sensible life and is constant in faith and love and holiness" (1 Timothy 2:15). He further defined the role of both a bishop and a deacon in such a way as to rule out women. The leaders of the Church were to be picked from among those males who ruled their households well, to say nothing of being the husbands of only one wife (1 Timothy 3:2). The author of Ephesians exhorted the wives to submit themselves to their husbands as unto the Lord, "since, as Christ is head of the Church… so is a husband head of his wife" (Ephesians 5:23).

So far as the Church could speak with authority, it proceeded to snuff out the early spirit of inclusive freedom and to lay a theological foundation which would establish beyond debate the secondary, subservient role and worth of women. In the name of a masculine God and in accordance with the will of this masculine God, the all-male hierarchy of the Church had declared it to be so. From this definition there was no court of appeal. By making that claim good, the door was open in Western Christian civilization from that moment on for men alone to define not only God and human life but also to order worship, to establish sacred tradition, and to build the theological boundaries around orthodoxy without ever hearing, much less responding to, whatever insights women might possess.

The reasons for the additional shift against women toward the end of the first century of Church history are not certain, but the reality is. One possible explanation is that Christianity began to move up the social ladder from the lower to the middle class. In the lower classes the labour of anyone able to work was needed, so the value of the woman could not be ignored. That pattern, in fact, still prevails even today in the Middle East, where only middle class women, not working women, are required to be veiled.[8]

Elaine Pagels, in her provocative book, *The Gnostic Gospels*, offers another possible explanation.[9] The Gnostic groups with whom the orthodox Christians appeared to be in competition, were universally more open to women than the dictates of the tradition and social order would tolerate. In the battle for supremacy which the orthodox bodies won, thereby winning for themselves the orthodox title, there was a general denigrating of any value associated with the Gnostics. Some Gnostic Christians and the orthodox Christians divided on their definition of God, with the Gnostics viewing God as a dyad having both male and female elements. In the Gnostic Gospel According to the Hebrews, Jesus spoke of "my mother, the Spirit".[10] The hebrew word *ruach*, which was translated 'spirit', was, in fact, a feminine word. In *The Gospel of Thomas*, Jesus contrasted his earthly parents, Joseph and Mary, with the Divine Father of Truth and the Divine Mother, the Holy Spirit.[11] *The Gospel of Philip* ridiculed those the author considered literal-minded Christians who mistakenly referred the virgin birth to Mary. "When did a woman conceive by a woman?", the author asks. "Christ was born from the Virgin Spirit", through the will of the Father, he asserted.[12]

These Gnostic writings were rigorously attacked by the guardians of orthodoxy, and the fact that the Gnostic groups seemed to have a powerful appeal to women, as noted even by Irenaeus,[13] caused the orthodox attack to have increasingly militant sexist overtones. The Gnostics were accused of being seducers of foolish women and purveyors of immoral actions. When the smoke of battle cleared, the Gnostics had been routed, and with them the liberalising attitude toward women in the Church may have been destroyed. Tertullian spoke for what was to become the orthodox attitude when he wrote, "It is not permitted for a woman to speak in the Church, nor is it permitted for her to teach, nor to baptize, nor to offer the Eucharist, nor to claim for herself a share in any masculine function, least of all in priestly office."[14]

The force of this statement indicates once again that women had, in fact, claimed for themselves each of the roles that Tertullian prohibited. No one prohibits that which no one had thought to do. But once the prohibition was pronounced, the justifying reasons were found and articulated. Inevitably the denigrating of the sexuality of women as something evil, unclean and unworthy was offered to buttress the decision against inclusiveness. With this negativity abroad, it was not long before the Church structures, traditions, theology and liturgy all possessed a deeply pervasive anti-female bias.

One has only to scratch the surface just a bit to find that this negativity toward women was loaded time after time on the experience of menstruation. An unspoken argument against female ordination was and is the ancient fear of menstruation's power to pollute. This fear was recounted endlessly in medieval books. In many parts of the Catholic Church, little girls and old women have been allowed to help in minor ways at Church functions, while women in their prime have not.[15] The implication is clear. Even into this century some Churches have taught that menstruating women were not to attend and receive Holy Communion. Jerome wrote, "Nothing is so unclean as a woman in her periods. What she touches she causes to be unclean."[16] The ancient prejudice had clearly found expression in the new religion. Christianity inherited misogyny as a given, and baptised this anti-female bias into its ongoing life. Christianity modified this negativity from time to time, but never really escaped it.

The major Christian contribution to the prevailing and inherited sexual attitudes came through a school of philosophy known as Manichaeism. This philosophical system, which was related to the Gnostic tradition,[17] emerged out of the Greek world but was grafted and incorporated so deeply into Christianity that people thought it was of the essence of the gospel. Manichaeism added a new dimension of negativity toward women, and it had a marked impact upon both the Church and the social order.

The philosophy of the Manichaeans was based on the popular Greek dualistic view of reality that elevated what it called the realm of the spirit and denigrated what it called the realm of the material or physical. The spiritual aspect of human life represented the higher self, the source of lofty and pure thoughts. The physical aspect of human life represented the lower self, the body, the source of base and carnal desires. This dualistic philosophy tended to divide the human being at the diaphragm, pronouncing that which was above the diaphragm, good, and that which was below the diaphragm, evil.

This point of view entered Christianity most specifically by way of Augustine, Bishop of Hippo, who had himself been a Manichaean philosopher prior to his conversion. Augustine was the most powerful and influential Christian thinker and teacher for a thousand years, so his impact was vast. But the

71

basic dualism of Manichaeism was also a pervasive and dominant attitude of Greek philosophy throughout the ancient world, and it interacted with Christianity at many points. It was the Manichaean attitude which fed and continues to feed that ascetic tradition in Christianity that suggests that the Christian life can be achieved only when the physical body has been mortified of its desires and the sinful world has been escaped in the quest to find God.

Not surprisingly, when this ascetic tradition talked about the flesh, it found sin most devastatingly present in human sexuality. Furthermore, it identified the sensuous power and attraction of this evil experience primarily with the female of the species. If sex was evil, then that creature who was the desired object of sexual temptations had to be evil. Clearly one sees that the value system out of which these judgments proceeded was designed by men. Were it not for the woman's seductiveness and her tempting power, then the lordly male would not fall under her evil spells and therefore might escape the sins of the flesh.

A breviary of love originating in AD 1288 put this concept into specific words when it said, "Satan in order to make men suffer bitterly, makes them adore women, for instead of loving... the creator... they sinfully love women".[18] These sentiments, informed by Manichaeism, constituted one more strand of the anti-women mentality that fed Western civilisation through the Christian Church. It is not yet the whole answer, but its presence must be isolated and noted in any attempt to understand the broad and deep negativity that the West has historically felt toward the female.

Those who are uncomfortable admitting this anti-female bias which has come through the Church, offer as a counter-argument that the importance given to Mary, the mother of our Lord, in Christian history tempered the negativity toward women in Western civilisation. A closer look at Mary, however, calls this theory into serious question. The Virgin Mary that we meet in the tradition and in the mythology of the Western Catholic world is consistently man's version of what a woman should be. Mary is woman defined, circumscribed and idealised by men who accept without questioning a particular male orientation. The male prejudice against women was so deep and so intense that their version of the ideal woman was both dehumanized and desexed, and only by this process could she achieve that ideal status of female perfection. Women would never have defined woman this way.

Mary's humanity was irrevocably compromised by the assertion that she was immaculately conceived and bodily assumed. These two doctrines suggested that her entrance into life and her departure from life were abnormal and unhuman. She was rather a special visitor to the earth, not a part of the woof and warp of life. Her female sexual capability was removed from her by the stories of her virgin birth and the later tradition of her perpetual virginity. Even wilder stories circulated to build ever greater barriers around her potential sexuality. One legend suggested that her impregnation by the Holy Spirit was through her ear. Another suggested that the birth of our Lord was through her navel. Female sexuality had to be very evil to the minds of those who produced these myths and traditions.

Only one sexual function was allowed Mary in Western history, and even that proved to be short-lived. The breasts of Mary could produce milk. She could lactate, and to this product of her body were ascribed remarkable therapeutic powers. An analysis of the medieval suckling stories about Mary show the gentle blending of many ancient goddess traditions of the pre-Christian world. The first nursing goddess appears to have been Isis in Egypt, 1000 years before Christ. Later, in Greek mythology the goddess Juno's milk was sprayed across the heavens one night while she was nursing Hercules. Because of this accidental spilling in the Greek myth, we call the heavenly bodies to this day the Milky Way; and even the word galaxy comes from the root *lac*, which means 'milk'. In the thirteenth century, phials in which Mary's milk was preserved were venerated all over Christendom. John Calvin in his treatise on relics said, "There is no town so small or convent so mean that it does not display some of the Virgin's milk. There is so much that if the Holy Virgin had been a cow or a wet nurse all her life, she would have been hard put to yield such a great quantity."[19]

Finally, however, even this human, sex-related quality in Mary was repressed, and stories about the healing milk of Mary faded from the tradition. Sin, according to the Garden of Eden story, was punished in the woman by childbirth (Genesis 3:16). In the era before prepared baby formulas, nursing was an essential part of the childbearing experience. There was no continuity of life without breastfeeding. As the stories of Mary's sinlessness began to circulate, inevitably the stories of any sex-related function, including nursing, became inappropriate. The only survival of this tradition today is the popular German wine, *Liebfraumilch*, which literally means 'dear lady's milk'. The only indication of a bodily function left in the humanity of Mary was her ability to shed tears, and tears became the only product of her body that was not repressed. Somehow in our strange, negative heritage we seem to believe that everything that comes out of the woman's body save for tears is evil.

The popular suggestion that devotion to Mary was translated into respect or enhanced status for women is simply without historical evidence. To the contrary, the Church Fathers who were extolling the virtues of the Virgin Mary were at the same time lambasting the sexuality of female persons. Tertullian in the third century and Chrysostom in the fourth century could be quoted at length. There is no historical correlation between the cult of the Virgin and increased status for women that can be substantiated in Western history. Mother Church was, in fact, ruled by men; and Mary served the desires of those men who created this holy ideal of what they thought all women should be and then imposed it on their women.

Mary's chief role was that of intercessor, which was also, not surprisingly, the special role of the mother in medieval patriarchal family life. The mother was never the judge. She never made the power decisions. The judge was always the husband and father, who was the source of power, authority and discipline. The mother's sole function was to intercede. She could plead for mercy in the handing down of punishment; but her only real power lay in her ability to move the lordly male to compassion and pity. The power structure of this family scene in medieval life was simply transposed in theological circles to the heavenly courtroom where the divine judge stood ready to punish sinners for their evil deeds. To ameliorate the sentence, the guilty party, reduced to childlike terror before the parental authority, would plead with the compassionate divine mother to pray to her son, the judge, on behalf of the penitent.

Marina Warner in her provocative book, *Alone of All Her Sex*, suggests that there is a historical correlation between the popularity of Mary and the low status of women even today.[20] In those countries where Mary still dominates the religious tradition of the people, the men still swagger and command and the women are more prone to submit and to withdraw. Machismo, Warner asserts, is the flip side of the sweet and gentle Mary who is not the ideal woman at all but the male ideal of what the submissive, powerless female should be.

Certainly the role of the woman in childbirth was recognised in Christian history by the Church Fathers, but they related to childbirth in a rather unusual way. Procreation was a necessary evil that ought to be escaped, they seemed to think. Their reasoning process went like this: women were inferior, so any attempt to elevate women had to be accomplished by removing the woman's sexuality, which was that human condition to which female inferiority was attached. This removal could be achieved only if women denied their sexuality. To express or to live out female sexuality was to carry on the sentence imposed on women in the Garden of Eden. So Cyprian, Tertullian and Jerome urged women to remain virgins "so that you will not suffer the consequences of the Fall."[21]

The early theologians wrote extensively on the joys available to women in the single life. There was no husband to obey, nor a pregnancy to endure. The sorrows of conception could be escaped and the marital condition could be avoided. Jerome asserted that only virginity could reverse woman's fall from grace in the Garden of Eden. He went on to say, "When a woman wishes to serve Christ more than the world, she will cease to be a woman and will be called a man."[22]

The importance of virginity hinged on the understanding of the female body generally abroad among the early Church Fathers. The virgin body was perfect and whole. Virginity, the status to which a woman was born, was created by God and

75

was therefore holy. Ambrose suggested that for a woman to lose her 'maidenhead' was to deface the work of the creator.[23] Marriage was tolerable, said Jerome, "only because more virgins were born as the result".[24] The Church Fathers made virginity the supreme image of wholeness and equated wholeness with holiness. Virginity thus was the only thing that separated humanity from the beasts.[25]

Sexual union was believed to destroy the virgin body.[26] One vestige of this idea remains in that the French today call orgasm, *la petite mort*, which means 'little death'. Chastity thus became the only effective means available to a woman to combat the evil of her sex, and childbearing became the only possible compromise with human sexuality. The dualism of the Manichaeans was assumed and unquestioned.

If a woman chose marriage over virginity, part of the legitimate price she had to pay was submission to her husband, who ruled her by the same divine right that kings claimed over their domains. "Every man a king in his own home", is not a slogan of recent political origin,[27] but rather the experience of women historically in Western civilisation. The Church proclaimed that the woman who aspired to be ideal would be docile, gentle and passive. After all, the ideal woman, the perpetual Virgin Mary, had responded to the annunciation, "Be it done unto me according to your will", and that response became the required attitude the married woman had to assume toward her husband. Sex was allowable in marriage only for the purpose of procreation. Women were not only inferior, but childbearing was a divine, necessary punishment they alone had to bear. Negativity toward sex was so great that sexual relations for any purpose other than childbearing was an unthinkable abomination. The condemnation of birth control today is a modern expression of this same attitude.

Through every medium this definition of woman was enforced by the Church. Of the classical theological virtues only charity has historically been applied to women, not the more vigorous virtues of faith or hope. Of the cardinal virtues only prudence seems to have a feminine characteristic, not fortitude or justice or temperance. To be feminine was to be passive. This passivity was acted out both in the symbolic marriage to Jesus—which was the ideal that led to the life of cloistered obedience of the virgin nun—and in the actual marriage to a man for the sole purpose of bearing children and obediently serving the man's needs and comfort. This latter alternative, while allowable, was at best thought to be a compromise with sin and the flesh.

Women thus could serve husbands and children as wives and mothers, or they could serve priests and children as nuns. No other options were available. Thus the Church has imposed its sexual stereotypes on the secular order. Here they have remained in force as the common folk wisdom long after the institutional power of the Church has waned. The Church's definition of women was operative in 1873 when the Supreme Court of the United States of America declined by an 8-1 vote to allow a woman named Myra Bradford to practise law in the state of Illinois. Listen to the nuances of a strongly-worded concurring opinion written by Justice Joseph P. Bradley:

> Man is or should be women's protector and defender. The natural and proper timidity and delicacy which belongs to the female sex evidently unfits it for many of the occupations of civil life. The constitution of the family organization which is founded in the divine ordinance as well as in the nature of things indicates the domestic sphere as that which properly belongs to the domain and function of womanhood. The paramount destiny and mission of woman are to fulfil the noble and benign office of wife and mother. This is the law of the creator. And the rules of civil society must be adapted to the general constitution and cannot be based upon exceptional cases.[28]

Justice Bradley certainly did not think of himself as anything but an 'objective' judge, and yet his sexual assumptions were the products of his religious heritage.

The secular order is in the process of challenging the sexual assumptions of the past and freeing itself from the power of those assumptions. But in many branches of the Christian Church, they still reign supreme and in some instances are even as yet unquestioned. The hard line still followed in many Church circles against the emergence of women from the stereotypes of the past arises from a historic inability of parts of the Christian movement to see women primarily as persons and not simply as creatures defined only by their sexuality as either virgins or baby-making machines.

Marina Warner, who was raised as a Roman Catholic, concludes *Alone of All Her Sex* by stating that the Vatican's inability to see women as people rather than mothers "underpins the Church's continuing indefensible ban on contraception; a dualistic distaste for the material world reinforces the ideal of virginity; and an undiminished certainty that women are subordinate to men continues to make the priesthood of women unacceptable".[29]

The force of this long-standing and powerfully held position is massive. Social systems and social attitudes that are this immense point to an equally immense fear and force that have to be mastered and controlled. We in this rational, civilised and enlightened era have not yet escaped these subliminal anxieties.

More than any of us recognise, we still harbour these ancient prejudices, and we still victimise women in the service of these prejudices. Look at some of the symbols we employ. A sexual success is called a conquest, as if in the nature of a war. Religious voices in our day have been raised in support of what is called 'traditional family values', but when that expression is defined by its advocates, it quickly loses its facade and is revealed as an anti-woman movement attached to traditional religious language. 'Traditional family values' seems to be a modern version of the argument that "a woman's place is in the home". Church-related groups in the United States were most vocal in opposition to the Equal Rights Amendment, and they are highly emotional in opposition to abortion.

When Sandra Day O'Connor was nominated for a position on the United States Supreme Court, there were strange negative things said publicly about women. In a letter to the editor of *TIME*, one Sheila Walker from Colorado commented succinctly, "The new right will never be satisfied with any female appointed to the judiciary. Obviously a woman who respects 'traditional family values' would not have gone to law school or sought a career outside the home."[30]

Many of our marriage customs still reflect these suppositions of the ages. What are we saying in the wedding ceremony when one man gives the woman away to another man? Does this not imply that the woman is a piece of property that can be bartered or exchanged? Why is the groom not given away?

Our economic structures reveal a continuing active bias against women. In medicine the overwhelming number of doctors are male while the females are the helpful and less well paid nurses. In business most executives are male, and the females are the indispensable but less well paid secretaries. In the field of education the superintendents and principals are overwhelmingly male, while females still constitute the large majority of the essential but less well paid teachers. Males are still primarily the dentists and the lawyers; females are the less well paid oral hygienists and legal assistants. The priesthood is overwhelmingly male, while faithful women prepare the altars where the priest celebrates the Eucharist and keep the priestly vestments clean and well-pressed.

We still castigate males when we perceive what we think of as female characteristics in them. Our profanity and our sex talk are filled with crude and vulgar hostility that express a still-present subliminal negativity toward women. Sexist prejudice is enormous, and in many ways its major generator in history has been nothing less than the Christian Church. We may well be able to trace these attitudes to their source, but we have yet to break their power over our minds.

These facts pose a major question for Christians involved in the contemporary revolution of social consciousness. Can this same Church which gave and still gives substance and value to these sexual stereotypes now free itself from these stereotypes and help us to enter a new era of freedom without destroying itself in the process?

To me, this question points to incredibly important issues that may well carry with them the very future existence of Christianity. I am convinced that the ordination of women to the priesthood in various parts of the Anglican communion is the tip in an enormous reformation that offers a tiny new hope that the Church might yet be able to survive and live in the brave new world of consciousness that is developing.

But the Church as we know it will never be the same if

that transition is accomplished. Sexual assumptions that are deep and still operative will have to be changed. Traditional role-enforcing mythologies will have to be abandoned. The Virgin Mary will have to be transcended and transformed so radically that her perpetual virgin status may well be seen as a sexist liability rather than a virtue. The ecclesiastical power formulas of the past will have to be rethought. The Church has a choice to make, perhaps more serious than it has ever before had to make. If the Church actively or passively insists on preserving or defending the attitudes of the past, if it has not within itself the courage to enter this new world of sexual consciousness, then it must retire from history. Inevitably, then, the quest for freedom from the sexual stereotypes of the past will move so far beyond the Church that it will become an antiquated group of guerilla fighters isolated in forgotten pockets, wondering why they are ignored and asking what happened to their cause. Our constituent members will be only those who could not embrace these changes.

In my view there is no way the clock of sexual stereotyping will ever be turned back—not by the Vatican, or the religious right, or the scared conservative Christians in every branch of Christendom—though in the short run they will be much more secure in that stance than will those of us who will move ahead.

I cast my vote for a dangerous future. In that future we Christians must enter and embrace incredible changes, bear the dislocations of traditions, endure the death of symbols, and find the freedom to escape the debilitating prejudices and taboos of all those ages which have bound our consciousness and ill-equipped us for the revolution we now face. The greatest upheaval in Christian history, I believe, confronts us in the next century.

1. Fritjof Capra, The Tao of Physics, Shambhala, Berkeley, 1975, p. 90.
2. Geoffrey Parrinder, Sex and the World's Religions, Oxford University Press, New York 1980, p. 117.
3. Marina Warner, Alone of All Her Sex: The Myth and the Cult of the Virgin Mary, Weidenfield and Nicolson, London, 1976, p. 177.
4. Aristotle, The Politics, I. II. 9. 11–12, ed. H. Rackman, London, 1949, quoted in Warner, p. 178.

5. *Since being a witness to the Resurrection was the only New Testament criterion for being an apostle, Mary Magdalene clearly qualified and may thus be considered the first woman in apostolic succession.*

6. *B. Brooten in* Women Priests: A Catholic Commentary on the Vatican Declaration, *eds. Leonard & Arlene Swidler, Paulist Press, New York, 1977, pp. 141–4.*

7. *Wayne Meeks,* The Image of Androgyne, *pp. 180ff, quoted in Elaine Pagels,* The Gnostic Gospels, *Random House, New York, 1979, p. 61.*

8. *In the Moslem fundamentalist revival in Iran, after the fall of the Shah, all women were required to be veiled.*

9. *Pagels, p. 63ff.*

10. *ibid. p. 52.*

11. *ibid.*

12. *ibid. p. 53 (The Gospel of Philip, 55: 25–6).*

13. *ibid. p. 53.*

14. *Tertullian,* De Virginibus Velandis, *9, quoted in Pagels, p. 60.*

15. *Warner, p. 76.*

16. *ibid.*

17. *The Rt Rev. C. FitzSimons Allison, former Virginia Seminary Church History Professor, says, "If Gnosticism is a dog, Manichaeism is a cocker spaniel".*

18. *Matfrè Ermengands,* Le Breviarai d'Amor, *2:148, ed. G. Agais, quoted in Warner, p. 153.*

19. *John Calvin,* Treatise on Relics, *quoted in Warner, p. 200.*

20. *Warner, pp. 183ff.*

21. *ibid. p. 73.*

22. *Jerome,* Commentary On Ephesians, *quoted in Mary Daly,* The Church and the Second Sex, *Harper & Row, New York, 1968, p. 43.*

23. *Ambrose,* Exhortatio Virginitatis, *quoted in Robert Briffault,* The Mothers, *Macmillan, New York, 1931.*

24. *Jerome,* Letter 22 to Eustochium, *quoted in Philip Schaff & Henry Wace, eds,* Nicene and Post-Nicene Fathers, *Series 2, Vol. 6: St Jerome,* Eerdmans, Grand Rapids.

25. *Mary Douglas,* Purity and Danger: An Analysis of the Concepts of Pollution and Taboo, *Routledge, London, 1966, pp. 186ff.*

26. *Warner, p. 72.*

27. *This was a major theme in George Wallace's 1972 presidential campaign in the USA.*

28. *Joseph P. Bradley, Concurring Opinion, US Supreme Court, 1873, Bradford vs. State of Illinois.*

29. *Warner, p. 338.*

30. TIME, *Letters to the Editor, vol. 118, no. 6, 10 August 1981.*

The Portrayal
of Women in the
Lectionary

Marie Louise Uhr

arjorie Proctor-Smith has examined the American Common Lectionary for the images of women it portrays and has discussed some of the effects these images may have on women.[1] This Common Lectionary was published in 1983 after five years work by scholars of most North American Churches: United Methodist, Lutheran, Presbyterian, Episcopal and Catholic. As the Church in Australia is still using an older lectionary, it seemed to me that it might be valuable to examine this earlier lectionary, which differs particularly in the readings chosen from the Old Testament, to see how women are portrayed and to consider what effects this might be having on the women of Australia.

As scripture readings are an important part of liturgical worship, the character of our worship depends significantly on what parts of scripture are included in the lectionary. The parts of scripture chosen for the lectionary, especially those to be read on Sundays and major feast days, not only make up major parts of our common worship but also become central parts of the teaching process of liturgy. Liturgical readings teach both by the outright exhortations they contain and also by the way the readings hold up models of good behaviour, of people living the way God wants us to live. The unspoken exhortations that these models give us are often more powerful than are the outspoken messages and commands. They implant in us images of what we should be and what is a good life. And the more these values are unspoken, the more we are likely to make them our own. So it is necessary to examine not only what the readings say about women, but also, and perhaps even more carefully, what models of virtuous women we are given.

All the scriptures, both Old and New Testament, are the products of patriarchal cultures. Hence we cannot be surprised to find that males have the dominant roles and that the text deals mainly with men. We cannot change that. Passages for inclusion in the lectionary, however, are selected and equal weight does not have to be given to all parts of scripture. The messages given in the liturgy will depend on which passages are chosen. And it is important to remember that the process of selection is itself a theological exercise and the results are a statement of values. So in the passages that are chosen for our lectionary, what part do women play? What values are being expressed? What do these passages say about women and about the role of women in salvation history?

The absence of women in most of the passages chosen for the lectionary and the silencing of their voices in passages in which they do appear, would seem to suggest that the answer to these questions is that women are of little value and play no significant part in salvation history.

An examination of readings chosen from the Old Testament for the liturgies of Sundays and major feast days shows that readings have been primarily selected to foreshadow and fore-tell the coming and the actions of the Messiah. First there are readings from the prophets. Second, readings are chosen which can be used to draw parallels between Old Testament and New Testament events so that Jesus can be seen to be the fulfilment of Israel's history. In addition, other readings are used which recount events of salvation history which empha-sise several male figures, particularly Abraham and Moses, through whom God is seen to have brought 'his' people to redemption. No woman is the major actor in any text chosen for a Sunday or major feast throughout the three-year cycle.

A clear example of the way in which the women are por-trayed is found in readings selected from the story of Sarah and Abraham. In them, Sarah appears twice as a character in the drama but is never allowed to speak. The two sections in which she appears are selections which culminate in the statement that Sarah and Abraham will have a son (I shall return to this point below). A silent Sarah, an acquiescent and passive Sarah, is certainly not the Sarah we find in Genesis, where she is active and in command. But all this authority and assertiveness are omitted from passages used in the liturgy.

Again, Moses speaks and acts in nearly thirty readings in the three-year cycle. But the women whose actions saved the infant Moses are ignored; no Shiphrah, no Puah, with their act of civil disobedience without which there would have been no adult Moses; no sister nor Egyptian princess who together reached across barriers of race and class to nurture the child;[2] only the fully-grown Moses speaking with God and leading the people.

The message is that Moses is important; the women are insignificant. In contrast, I would suggest that stories of people reaching across barriers of race and class and stories of people gently and bravely ignoring the lethal dictates of tyrants, are critical to our very survival today and have more to tell us than do stories of the founding of nations, even of the nation of Israel.

Who are the women whose voices we hear? The only female voices we hear in the Old Testament readings (apart from that of Eve) are those of three women: the widow of Sidon who speaks with Elijah (1 Kings 17:10-16, used on the 32nd Sunday of Year B, and 1 Kings 17:17-21, 10th Sunday of Ordinary Time in Year C); the Shumannite woman who befriended Elisha (2 Kings 4:8-11, 14-16, 11th Sunday of Ordinary Time in Year A); and Hannah (1 Samuel 1:20-2, 24-8, Feast of the Holy Family in Year C). The common theme throughout the stories of these three women is the granting to them of the life of a son in return for their love, generosity, hospitality and prayer. Both Hannah and the Shumannite woman are told that they will have a son; the widow of Sidon already has a son when her story opens; this son is restored to life by the action of Elijah. As noted earlier, the birth of a son is also the emphasis in the readings from the story of Abraham and Sarah.

No doubt the Israelite people regarded the birth of a son as a great gift from God, and of much more importance than the birth of a daughter. Moreover, the compilers of the lectionary were probably concerned with drawing parallels between the birth of these sons (or the raising of them to life) and the birth of Jesus and his bringing of God's life to us. But I question the wisdom today of choosing to feature stories of women which culminate in the giving to them of a son, rather than stories which celebrate the lives and actions of women. Moreover, I question the wisdom of this emphasis on the gift of a son as God's greatest gift. Not only does it seem to deny the value of a daughter, but it proclaims that a woman's prime role is producing children, and that her fulfilment comes from that alone.

The single and childless women of our communities find this insistent emphasis on children as a woman's (not a man's) fulfilment to be very painful. Is it any wonder that there is a demand for an in vitro fertilisation program when the Church continues to preach that the destiny and fulfilment of a woman's existence comes in the birth of a son?

There is a second point about the readings chosen from the stories of these three women which is equally important. Perhaps because it was essential to the compilers that the giving of a son was included in the readings, other parts of the stories are omitted. To me these omissions are tragic. For example, in the readings from the story of Hannah, the lectionary omits her marvellous statement, "I was pouring out my soul before Yahweh... I have been speaking from the depth of my grief and my resentment" (1 Samuel 1:15-16).[3] This omission means that she is unable to be heard as a model of a person engaged in open, deeply human prayer to God, prayer in which all our human feelings can be expressed. I think we need this model. Most of us have trouble with prayer and with being open with God and with one another.

Or again, in the readings from the story of the Shumannite woman, Elisha is heard wishing to thank her for her hospitality. In the text (2 Kings 4:13), Elisha first asks her "Is there anything you would like said for you to the king or the commander of the army?" Isn't this saying: "Would you like me to put in a good word for you to those who hold political and military power in this country?" She rejects this replying: "I live with my own people about me". A woman is offered political and military might; she rejects it. This rejection is omitted from the lectionary readings which jump to Elisha's second offer in which he promises the woman a son. Here again a woman is not allowed to be seen as a person for whom being part of the structures of worldly power is not simply unnecessary, but is to be rejected; again a lesson I think we need today.

The use of the stories of the creation of Adam and Eve was not altered in the development of the Common Lectionary, and so these sections have been analysed by Proctor-Smith. In summary, she shows that Adam's creation is portrayed as an essential part of salvation history, while Eve's creation is linked with the institution of marriage. The central message is clear. Men are the actors of salvation history. Women are wives and mothers.

In the selections chosen from the New Testament, the Common Lectionary and the older lectionary in use in Australia are very similar; again the analysis by Proctor-Smith is pertinent to our liturgy. But it must be noted that the Australian lectionary includes readings of the Graeco-Roman household codes[4] in both Years A and B. Colossians 3:12–21, which has been omitted from the Common Lectionary, is used in Year A on the feast of the Holy Family; Ephesians 5:21–32 is used on the 21st Sunday of Ordinary Time in Year B. Both readings state that wives should submit to their husbands. The reading from Colossians also includes the instruction to children to "be obedient to your parents always", but stops, as does the Ephesians reading, before the instruction that slaves "be obedient to the men who are called your masters in this world". These calls for submission, this insistence on dominance-submission patterns in human relationships, support the belief that males are heads of households, that their word is law and that it is God who demands this relationship.

Indeed the use in the liturgy of this reading from Ephesians seems to me to be very dangerous for women because the author parallels God's position over the Church with the husband's position over his wife: it says that as "Christ loved the Church... *and made her clean... in the same way* husbands must love their wives" (my emphasis). This is open to the interpretation that a husband's love and domination will make a normally-dirty woman clean and whole. How much wife-battering and incest have followed from the Church's continuing to give head-of-household power to men and to give it in the name of God? Will we ever know?

In the Gospel readings at last we find women acting, speaking, being primary actors in the drama, and ministering and being ministered to. In spite of this, we find again, as Marjorie Proctor-Smith has detailed, the tendency for the compilers to omit the ministering of women during recital of the passion narratives. The message would seem to be that the witness of women to the passion, death and burial of Jesus is not critical to this central story of our faith. I am not suggesting that these omissions are deliberate acts to degrade women and deny their ministry. I believe that these selections are made by people who cannot possibly know the pain their actions cause to so many women.

We need to examine carefully the selections from scripture that are used liturgically. The selections used in Australia could be said, at best, to legitimate the view that women are nothing but wives and mothers. At worst, they are seen to picture women as irrelevant to salvation history. This image of women as passive and unimportant is one with which women have seemed to acquiesce. Because it is the most common image of women that both women and men have, women have accepted this portrayal of themselves as valid and have allowed themselves to be submissive; they have internalised the judgements of them made, consciously or unconsciously, by others. This image of the passive subordinate woman is strongly reinforced by the passages of scripture selected for the lectionary and read to women and men each Sunday as "the Word of the Lord".

I would suggest, too, that the apparent unimportance of women in salvation history is reinforced by the total omission from the Sunday lectionary of any the biblical stories of horror committed against women, stories which have been so brilliantly brought to life by Phyllis Trible in her book *Texts of Terror*.[5] These stories live in our scriptures, but with no memorial of mourning in our liturgies, they remain as silent stones signifying the unimportance of women. In our Judaeo-Christian tradition, the sacrifice of the life of the daughter of Jephthah carries none of the theological significance of the offering up of the life of Isaac. But it remains for women as a terrible memorial of what can be done to women—to others—in the name of God.

In summary, the selections of our scriptures used in the lectionary for the liturgies of Sundays and major feast days, portray women as insignificant to salvation history, and as of value only as wives and mothers. For the sake of both women and men, this must change. Women must be able to gain strength and courage from the lectionary, and, to do this, they need the stories of women which our scriptures contain but which have been largely ignored in the compilation of the lectionary.

It is not only women who need these stories. These stories contain powerful antidotes to some of the prevalent mores and values of our society. They show people choosing life over death, choosing to disobey laws which order killings, choosing to ignore the barriers of race, class and state which have brought hatred, wars and death; women of courage choosing the way of non-violence, women of courage saying 'no' to political power, women in touch with their emotions and unafraid to show them to God. Do we not need their help today, not just for our spiritual growth, but for the very survival of humanity?

This article was first printed in *St. Mark's Review*, 135, 22–5 (1988) and appears here with the kind permission of the Editor.

---

1. Marjorie Proctor-Smith, *'Images of Women in the Lectionary'*, Concilium 182: Women—Invisible in Theology and Church, *1985, eds E. S. Fiorenza & M. Collins, pp. 51-62* .
2. *Phyllis Trible*, Women's Work is Never Done, *Thatcher Lecture, Union Theological College, Sydney, 1986.*
3. *All translations in this article are from* The Jerusalem Bible, *Darton, Longman and Todd, London, 1966, which is the translation used in the Australian common lectionary.*
4. *See Elisabeth Schüssler Fiorenza,* In Memory of Her, SCM, London, 1983, pp. 245-70, *for a discussion of these codes and their use in scripture.*
5. *Phyllis Trible,* Texts of Terror, Fortress Press, Philadelphia, 1984.

Reflections on Priesthood in the Roman Catholic Church

Roberta Hakendorf

s the twentieth century speeds to a close, the Roman Catholic Church seems poised for great change. This essay focusses on the priesthood, the centrepiece of the present ecclesiastical system. The crisis in clergy numbers leads to reflection on the evolution and ascendancy of the priesthood with the corresponding diminution of the role of the Christian community. Future possibilities are canvassed. However, I wish to acknowledge the dedication and pastoral concern of priests both now and over the centuries, and my own debt to many.

In most Western countries, the shortage and advancing age of Roman Catholic clergy is evident; perhaps this is the most notable feature of the Church at this time. Australia is now feeling the pinch. In June 1987, Fr Iverson, President of St Patrick's College, Manly, New South Wales, said on ABC Radio that by the year 2000, Sydney will have half the number of priests it had in 1987. Geraldine Doogue in *The Shifting Heart* claimed that in 2000 there will be 110 parishes in Sydney without a priest and that the average age of priests will be 65.[1] Parishes without a school or hospital are already being warned that they may soon lose their priests. Other Australian States face a similar situation; increasing one-priest parishes, parish amalgamations and the occasional priestless parish.

In the United States, a study, *The Catholic Priest in the US*, sponsored by the bishops in 1990, expects a 40 per cent decline in the number of diocesan priests between 1966 and 2005; during this time, the Catholic population is expected to increase about 36 per cent.[2] The situation in Europe was serious as far back as the late 1970s when Jan Kerkhofs of *Pro Vita Mundi* warned that where the figure of 100 would represent complete replacement for 100 losses of priests through death or resignation, the Netherlands registered 8, France 17, Belgium 15, Germany 34, Italy 50, Ireland 45, Spain 35 and Portugal 10.[3] As for England, Alex Cosgrave began an article in *The Tablet*: "The clergy of England and Wales are getting old. Within the next decade this natural ageing process is likely to cause a major crisis in the Church." Many priests still on the active list were past statutory retiring age; many more would be 65 within the next five to 10 years. Vocations had remained "on a plateau" for ten years.[4] Seminarians decreased by half in the 1970s in Europe and North America, the exceptions being Poland and Yugoslavia. Australia is importing priests from Poland. Even in the Third World, where there is some increase in native clergy, this is often offset by decreasing numbers of foreign priests and increasing numbers of Catholics.

In 1987, *L'Osservatore Romano* reported on a survey from the Central Office of Church Statistics. This found that the mean age of priests world-wide had increased by two-and-a-half years, decreasing only in Africa and Asia. The Highest increase in mean age occurred in Europe, with four countries exceeding 60. In Canada, the increase was from 53.1 to 57.3 and in the USA from 49.8 to 53.3. The percentage of young priests has decreased everywhere, except in South America; the decrease in young priests is small in Africa, "but radical in North America, Continental Central America, Europe and Oceania". Correspondingly, ageing "has leaped in these countries".[5] The system cannot long survive this widespread shortage and ageing of priests, and people in the pews are becoming much more alert to the statistics.

This situation is comparable to that in the Roman Catholic school system, where lay teachers now form 90 per cent of the teaching staff; thirty years ago the staff was 100 per cent religious. A quiet revolution has occurred. A second is occurring with priests.

The major result of this priest shortage is the loss of Eucharist to millions. This deprivation has gone on for several centuries in the Third World, but now is hurting the West. In June 1988, the Congregation for Divine Worship regularised the situation by setting out guidelines for services when there is no priest to celebrate Sunday Mass. These are becoming known as 'priestless' or 'Eucharist-less' Sundays. However, the Christian community has the right to a full Eucharist which no ecclesiastical system can deny; scripture readings and distribution of preconsecrated hosts do not comprise the Eucharist. In the short-term, we face mass consecrations of hosts for such services, in an attempt to shore up the system.

Many other problems are arising in priestless parishes. Small communities risk destruction as some members travel to available Masses elsewhere; gradually, huge amalgamations of parishes may occur, swallowing several communities in the process. Life is difficult for the 'circuit-riding' priests, who service several parishes but end up belonging to none, thus breaking the essential link between priest and community; such priests can also become seriously over-extended. Conversely, parish assistants or associates and administrators become frustrated at not being able to provide a full sacramental service, as they do everything except this. Concern is expressed at this separation of pastoral and sacramental ministry; the priesthood may appear expendable. Finally, this trend seems to provide dispensation from the Sunday obligation. All of this could herald a non-sacramental stance in the Roman Catholic Church.

Clearly, then, the present ecclesiastical system is under great pressure. However, does the Church collapse without priests? Many Roman Catholics find it almost impossible to imagine the Church without priest and parish, because from the seventeenth and eighteenth centuries in France, and elsewhere, "the priest was placed in a mystical niche, exalted, described as metaphysically equal to, even higher than angelic beings. He lost his roots in the community and in the wider diverse Church".[6] Some painful demythologising of priesthood is essential in order to face and plan for a possibly priestless Church. Perhaps no better way to assist this process is to draw attention to the evolution of priesthood.

In the first century of Christianity there were no Christian priests and certainly none in the New Testament. Jesus was not a priest, nor was Paul, nor Peter. Jesus did not directly give us priests, bishops and popes, nor the present hierarchical system, and, with the sophisticated Jewish religious system at hand, it would have been easy for him to do so. There is no trace in the Gospels that Jesus mentioned the cultivation of cult, his only remotely cultic action being the Last Supper. I believe strongly, with Schillebeeckx, that if the Holy Spirit presided over the evolution of priesthood, then the same Spirit may well point the Church in a non-clerical direction in the twenty-first century.[7]

In Paul's Corinthian church, neither priest nor bishop was present. In his descending list of charisms, priesthood does not appear: "God has appointed in the Church... first apostles, secondly prophets, thirdly teachers... after them, miraculous powers, then gifts of healing, helpful acts, guidance, various kinds of tongues".[8] On a day-to-day basis, prophets occupied the highest places in the local congregations, as the Spirit spoke directly to them. The second century *Didache* indicates that they were also presidents of the Eucharist.

While it is not my purpose to set the charismatic Corinthian church in absolute opposition to other emerging structures, it should be noted that a second system operated in Jerusalem with presbyters, as in Acts and in the Pastoral Epistles (1 & 2 Timothy, Titus), in which there were *episkopoi* or bishops, with deacons, but these were not originally considered priests. In fact, Bernard Cooke makes clear that not even the monarchic bishops so central to Ignatius of Antioch's epistles were priests. The term 'priest' does not emerge until the middle of the second century, and then contrary to New Testament practice, according to Bernard Cooke, who is of the opinion that there was general reluctance to use the word right through until about the Council of Nicaea (AD 325).[9] Bishops were the presidents of the Eucharist in a collegial celebration with their presbyters, but even they only gradually acquired the title 'priest'. Gradually, too, presbyters attained an autonomous function in the Eucharist and the title, 'priest', especially as more widespread areas were to be serviced, which the bishop could not reach.[10] It is a historical fact that Old Testament notions of priesthood, especially from Leviticus, slowly exerted profound influence over early Christianity, one hesitates to say at variance with the New Testament. Bernard Cooke laments that the "radical newness", of Christianity was not held to more faithfully by second century Christians.[11]

Early on, the second model, with its monarchic bishop, priest and deacon, replaced the charismatic Corinthian church. Hans Küng finds it incredible that the Church order of the genuine Pauline epistles, especially 1 Corinthians, should have been set aside in favour of that of the much later Pastorals.[12] However, with the emergence of the office of bishop at the end of the first century, diversity of ministry shrivelled; prophets disappeared during the third century, as did teachers, both roles being drawn into the office of bishop, according to Cooke.[13] Küng draws attention to the fact that the Pastoral Epistles exhibit "a strongly emphasised theology of Church office".[14]

From the fifth century until Vatican II, all ministry in the Church was reduced from great diversity to a state of 'monoformity', according to O'Meara,[15] and uniformity, according to Küng[16]—that of priesthood only. The early Middle Ages witnessed an incredible entrenchment of clerical control. In 1179, the Third Lateran Council made annual Confession of sin to a priest obligatory, thus giving priests ultimate control over salvation itself. It is worth noting that individual Confession had come into vogue only as late as the sixth century, introduced by Irish monks. Prior to 751, Anointing of the Sick was administered by laity and clergy alike, with a clear preponderance for lay administration. By 1100, Anointing was reserved for the priest alone, as it involved forgiveness of sin. Likewise, prior to 751, Marriage did not involve clergy, but by 1000, the ministry of a priest was necessary for validity.[17] In the twelfth century, the number of sacraments, the official means of grace, was set at seven, and it was at this time, as Schillebeeckx points out, that the theory of a "mysterious sacramental character" was emerging, which would give rise sometimes to a "magical sacerdotalisation of the priesthood."[18]

For centuries in the Church, office has dominated charism; ordination has dominated charism; ordination has dominated baptism. Roman Catholics today must realise that charisms of the Spirit are not just found within the hierarchy of priests. The explosion of ministries since Vatican II is evidence of this.

However, the most powerful argument for the demythologising of priesthood is found in a study of the Eucharist. David N. Power reminds us that in third century Rome, liturgy was not as important a factor in dividing lay and cleric, as full-time Church administration.[19] Today, Mass-saying is almost the only difference between lay and cleric. Power points to a gradual institutionalisation of all liturgical ministries. This "formalisation or clericalisation of roles and ministries...

exclude[d] the laity from liturgical services", in contrast to the early centuries when the liturgy had been the concern of all.[20] He considers that the final seal on this development occurred in the fifth century when the anonymous Pseudo-Dionysius applied the neo-Platonic term 'hierarchy' to the ministry of the Church. In this hierarchical view of the whole of creation, each should keep the place assigned by God.[21] Power concludes that "the clergy did indeed 'overpower' the laity and ministries were monopolised".[22]

Originally, of course, the Eucharist was celebrated in the private homes of early converts until Constantine's *Edict of Toleration* in the fourth century, when large churches or basilicas came into use. Generally, increased distance from the Eucharistic action led to total passivity for the community. Joseph Jungmann, in *The Mass of the Roman Rite*, states that soon after the Eucharist moved into large buildings, the very architecture began to demonstrate that, "the line of separation between altar and people, between clergy and laity... was now made into a broad line of demarcation, not to say a wall of division".[23] The altar was moved back to the rear wall and finally a rood-gallery or choir, which sometimes became a real wall, separated the sanctuary from the nave of the church, demonstrating very accurately that the earlier, "conscious participation of the community in that oblation of Christ was lost sight of".[24]

These changes reflected official policy for the Third Lateran Council; the Fourth, in 1215, ushered in absolute ordination by declaring that now only valid ordination was required for presidency of the Eucharist. Calling by the community, as in the first millennium, was thus set aside. The Fourth Lateran Council stated that "only a validly ordained priest can speak the words of consecration".[25] Schillebeeckx points to the privatising, the individualising of priesthood beginning with these prescriptions.[26] Priesthood was being viewed as a state, not as a ministry to the community.

Emphasis shifted from the community as the Body of Christ to the bread and wine, and to the relationship of the leader to the food of the Eucharist. Even as far back as Justin Martyr, change was understood to be effected in the bread and wine;

97

an objectification, a reification was beginning. The Eucharist was being considered a thing, the consecrated bread and wine as the flesh and blood of Christ, rather than as an action, with the community offering and celebrating. As Joseph Powers sees it, a theology of confection was on its way, replacing the community's celebrating and thanksgiving. There was a certain shrinkage in the understanding of Eucharist to something which was celebrated by the one who presided rather than by the whole community, the Body of Christ.[27] There was greater concentration on the power of the priest over the bread and wine on the altar, power over Christ's presence. Priestly power could change bread and wine into Christ.

In early Christianity, the Eucharistic elements were never described as sacred objects but, as Guzie points out, they "gradually became sacred objects; what was known as the mystery of the Eucharist became a physical miracle". The notion of real presence came in and at a certain level of understanding, "real presence can only mean physical presence ... it is simply a body we can't see, and magic or a miracle is still needed", to put the 'body' with the bread and wine.[28] The problem was that attention shifted from the Eucharistic action involving the whole community to the elements on the altar. There was considerable concentration on change. To explain this, the Fourth Lateran Council opted for Transubstantiation, using Aristotle's categories to explain the change in the substance but not in the accidents, or appearances.

In the early Middle Ages, there was a change from ordinary bread to pure white unleavened wafers, which also ushered in the small paten over the chalice instead of the large platter for loaves of bread. The people's offertory procession went out, too. A further blow to the community was the placing of the host on the tongue, instead of in the communicant's hands, to prevent the laity touching it. Very slowly, according to Jungmann, the practice of kneeling to receive communion was introduced, as also a low communion rail, "calculated to broaden the moat between the faithful and the sanctuary".[29] Latin was the language of the liturgy, incomprehensible to all but the educated. Finally, only the priest was active, and the faithful were like spectators at a drama of the Way of the Cross.

From the ninth century, the Mass had been viewed as an allegory based on the Passion, every movement conforming to this. "The *eucharistia* has become an *epiphania*, an advent of God who appears amongst men and dispenses his graces."[30] The Christian was viewed as a mere passive recipient of grace, instead of as a member of a community intimately involved.

At this point, it is useful to reflect that in the earliest ordination ritual, Hippolytus' *Apostolic Tradition* of the third century, there is no mention of preaching or celebrating the Eucharist in the ordination rite for a presbyter—he was ordained simply to advise the *episcopos*.[31] Medieval practice moved a great distance from this. Almost certainly, the twenty-first century will witness even further evolution of the role of presidency of the Eucharist. All of the changes in the liturgy since the 1950s, but especially after Vatican II, have aimed at the restoration of the community: use of the vernacular, responses, the offertory procession, the priest facing the people, access to the chalice, bringing the altar closer to the people, communion in the hand and the liturgical ministries open to the laity. However, the process is by no means complete.

With the present Roman Catholic ecclesiastical system under threat because of its priest shortage, where does one look for an alternative which will restore the community to its ancient position? There are some marvellously positive signs in the Church. One is the number of lay persons, especially women, studying theology and scripture; many are seeking personal spiritual development; lay ministries are flowering in a new spring. However, one sign above all heralds a whole new way of being Church: new structures, a lay Church, with equal possibilities for all—women and men—based on baptism and the charisms of the Spirit. This single most optimistic sign is the world-wide proliferation since Vatican II of base communities, especially in South America. Almost certainly these will form the major unit of organisation in the future Roman Catholic Church.

Karl Rahner writes: "The Church of the future will be one built from below by basic communities as a result of free initiative and association. We should make every effort not to hold up this development but rather to promote it."[32] Gustavo Gutierrez speaks of "the irruption of the poor in Latin America", to describe the unprecedented movement of the poor, in their communities, into the life of the Church.[33] Until Vatican II, the Church formed part of the economic, social and political structures of oppression, but Jon Sobrino sees the Church now recovering some of the characteristics of Jesus, who had pity on the crowds, healed the sick and unmasked hypocrisy.[34] These communities first appeared in the 1960s and stemmed from the Church's opening of itself to the world through Vatican II, from the shortage of priests and from a massive struggle for justice. While some basic communities existed before the Medellin Conference (1968), after it the whole movement took off.

Each base community consists of about thirty families of poor people, not middle- or upper-class. Readings from the word of God lie at the heart of all meetings. Leadership is increasingly in lay hands. New ministries are emerging; increasingly, the sacraments of baptism and marriage are being celebrated by these leaders. However, Eucharists are infrequent and rely on a 'circuit-riding' priest who services several communities. Priestless Sunday liturgies are led by lay persons but are not full Eucharists. Some go ahead and celebrate the complete Eucharistic liturgy without a priest. Sessions for the training of leaders in scripture, theology, catechesis, first-aid and leadership skills are held three or four times a year. A pocket literature is developing. A team of leaders is preferred to the singular ministry of the priest.

However, the question must be asked: are the base communities Church, local Church, as Vatican II understood the term? The Medellin Document, *Joint Pastoral Planning,* gives the answer: "the Christian base community is the first and fundamental ecclesiastical nucleus... the initial cell of the ecclesiastical structures" (no. 10). In Sydney, in July 1990, Jose Marins emphasised the term 'basic ecclesial communities' and stressed that these are rooted historically in the early Christian communities of Corinth, Philippi, Ephesus, Antioch and Jerusalem. They are certainly not a mere innovative movement in the Church, and certainly not a new Church.[35]

While the size of today's parishes, dioceses and Sunday

100

congregations greatly inhibits their functioning as communities, the small base communities are effectively building Christian community, the Body of Christ, the People of God, as the Church of the first millennium understood itself. Australian Roman Catholics have experienced many types of small groups; nevertheless, those exhibiting an on-going dimension are really providing the foundation of future Church organisation. The Passionist Family Group Movement is an excellent example. There are others: the Christian Life Movement, Christian Life Communities, Review of Life, Lenten groups and Renew. There are base communities all through Western society, as Dr Ian Fraser emphasised during his visit to Adelaide in April 1990, and in his book, *Wind and Fire*.[36]

However, there is no Christian community without Eucharist. The base communities of the Third World are dramatically highlighting the greatest weakness in the present ecclesiastical system, for despite such marvellous life at the grass roots, not seen since the early centuries, they are largely without Eucharist because of the shortage of priests. Schillebeeckx asserts that a Christian community has the right to leaders and to Eucharist, the leaders being the presidents of Eucharist.[37] There are leaders in the base communities but because they are not celibate and seminary-trained, they are not allowed to preside at Eucharist. Millions are thereby deprived.

Karl Rahner suggests relative ordination, that is, the ordination of catechists or co-ordinators of a base community, for that community only.[38] Leonardo Boff suggests that perhaps a lay community co-ordinator could be consecrated as "an extraordinary minister of the celebration of the Lord's Supper", not ordained but able to provide Eucharist when a priest is absent.[39] However, as celibacy over the centuries has been a great wall separating clerics from laity, almost certainly this will never be breached by the present ecclesiastical system. In the short term, Eucharists will become less frequent, as the number of priests declines, but continued deprivation of Eucharist will not continue once participative structures are in place. Then a system will soon be found to provide Eucharist. Meanwhile, the Eucharistic problem alone is signalling the eventual demise of the present ecclesiastical system.

The base communities are therefore heralding a radical restructuring of the Church. Also, the present system will not be able to maintain itself as priestly numbers further diminish. Leonardo Boff speaks of the communities "re-inventing the Church", a renaissance, a "birthing of the Church" and starting the Church again. He says: "We are not dealing with the expansion of an existing ecclesiastical system, rotating on a sacramental, clerical axis, but the emergence of another form of being Church, rotating on the axis of the word of the laity... from this a new type of institutional presence of Christianity will emerge." Boff is not convinced that Jesus provided just one model of Church: "The base communities are calling into question the prevailing manner of being Church."[40]

Restructuring cannot be endlessly postponed. The base communities have evolved a decision-making process more accurately symbolised by concentric circles than the old pyramidal, hierarchical system, under pope, bishop and priest in descending order. Such a process has swept the people from passivity to active participation. Schillebeeckx sees the communities as the means by which the Church is prepared for the introduction of another Church order, "more suitable for the modern world and its pastoral needs."[41]

How to affect community-based Church government is the big question for the twenty-first century. Rahner does not consider that the Church should merely copy secular democracy but he insists on the "collaboration of Church people in the life of the Church and the decision of authority... [as they] are not merely recipients of what is done by the institutional Church but are themselves the Church." Participation must be more than informal; "it needs juridical and visible structures" to be made real.[42] Such participative structures would be enhanced if accompanied by Ignatian discernment.

The basic ecclesial communities are showing the way with a team of leaders and decisions reached by consensus, with all members participating. The initial decision for future restructuring is whether the base community will be the nucleus of the whole edifice, and whether clusters of these are to form a larger unit, but one smaller than the existing parish. Perhaps a number of clusters may make up a sub-region, smaller than a diocese; a group of sub-regions may comprise a region, all of these forming the national church. Whatever the shape of future church organisation, it is to be discerned by the whole membership under the guidance of the Holy Spirit, so that government from below results, not some imposition from above. The names to be given to the clusters and to the various leaders are a lesser matter to be worked out in time, some variation occurring among the virtually autonomous national churches to allow for cultural diversity. A team of leaders is much more likely than the mono-ministry of the priest in the present system.

Over twenty years ago, Schillebeeckx wrote: "Furthermore, even an episcopal or presbyterial structure of the leadership of the Church is not dogmatically inviolate",[43] and "There is no direct link between the contemporary offices of the Church (the episcopate, the presbyterate, and the diaconate) and an act of institution on the part of Jesus while he was on earth".[44] In a later *Concilium* article, he comments on the tendency in the Church "to identify old, even venerable traditions with unchangeable divine dispensations", especially in relation to the threefold division in holy orders. Schillebeeckx then draws attention to the fact that Vatican II merely referred to their origin 'from antiquity', not by *divina ordinatione*, as suggested in the Council of Trent.[45] The door is open to profound change. Widespread experimentation and flexibility is essential in the early stages, not one cast-iron system imposed. However, an organisationless future is certainly not envisaged.

The necessary background for restoration of the national churches is decentralisation from Rome, so that they can begin to resemble the great patriarchates of Rome, Antioch and Alexandria in the early centuries. However, the historical fact of increased centralisation on Rome, especially since the Reformation, should be clearly recognised before there can be any realistic understanding of where future church organisation may well go. The 'People of God' theology of Vatican II can never be more than theory without massive decentralisation, for the papacy is in reality still a monarchy which in its ascendancy greatly diminished the power of the national churches and their bishops. There followed, especially after the Reformation, demand for uniformity of liturgical rites, theology and moral practice. This tendency led to Papal Infallibility, the centralising of the teaching role in one person.

The full restoration of the national churches may most fittingly occur within a representational model, as in Patristic times, with the papacy becoming fully collegial and pastoral in orientation. Subsidiarity will be its hallmark, with as much decision-making as possible at the local level, especially the election of bishops. Collegiality may yet bring the still isolated papacy back to the College of Bishops. Paul VI's innovation, the Synod of Bishops, which is merely consultative, has tended to become a papal rubber stamp, unable either to set its own agenda or publish its own findings. Patrick Granfield suggests that the Synod needs to be raised to deliberative, decision-making status.[46] It is also dominated by the Curia, but with the national churches growing in autonomy, and managing their own affairs, the Curia should shrink in size and importance. Cardinals could well be dispensed with, as national church leaders will almost certainly elect future popes. Papal elections may also be modernised, putting aside the medieval drama still enacted. Nor need Rome be forever the hub of the Church; it would be most fitting for one of the South American churches to be the first to take this honour from Rome; any See in the future could be eligible.

The movement from centralism and absolute monarchy would correspondingly effect the concept of Papal Infallibility. As Rahner suggests, perhaps any future definitions may comprise only defense of, and up-to-date restating of "the basic substance of Christianity".[47] Indeed, as Ian Fraser foresees, there will be a much greater role for all, for the grass roots, in future theological exploration and restatement, without any devaluing of theologians.[48]

In the Church of the third millennium, Christian moral norms will be discerned by all, in small groups, and in clusters of groups, the results coming before the national and finally a universal council of the Church. General norms should be determined at the highest level, but their cultural expression at the regional level, for instance, the African church may permit polygamy. Sexual morality has been a most aggravating area since Vatican II, especially after *Humanae Vitae* in 1968 prohibited artificial contraception. The youth of today are disenchanted with the heavy weight of the Church's moral proscriptions.

Rome's sister churches will watch these developments and once they see effective collegiality and subsidiarity emerging, may well feel more inclined to join her in a loose fellowship or commonwealth, particularly if collegiality leads to a more participatory style of government. Voluntary renunciation of monarchic status by the popes would be a welcome sign, dispelling fear of Roman domination. Rome's ancient role as guardian of unity may re-emerge. Meanwhile, the pope would do well to have the Catholic Church join the World Council of Churches, and hold summits for all church leaders, thereby becoming an ecumenical pastor, as Granfield suggests, but with "a papal style that... shuns authoritarianism in every form".[49] Unfortunately, chapters one and two of *Lumen Gentium*, the major document of Vatican II, places two models of Church side-by-side: the hierarchical, with all power vested in the pope and in descending order—bishops and priests—and the second, the Church as a sacramental mystery and a community. A future council is very likely to remove this anomaly by officially returning from hierarchy to *communio*, the oldest model of Church—brought back to prominence by Yves Congar, prior to Vatican II.

It is fascinating to peer down the decades into the late twenty-first century Church. The nerve-centre of all this change will be the small group, its members nourished on Word and Sacrament—from their own hands. No longer are there lay/cleric dichotomies. Gone are the days of infrequent Eucharist and fill-in alternatives. Now, of course, when a cluster of small groups meets there is scope for a larger Eucharistic gathering, perhaps in the old parish church; similarly, when the sub-region and region meet. In this declericalised Church, where all are equal on the basis of baptism, the charism of leadership alone, not gender, will determine presidency of Eucharist. Leadership at every level will be open to all.

Many Roman Catholic women, myself included, do not wish to serve in the present structures where priests form a separate caste in the cultic mode. In the ecclesial communities of the future, once women are seen to possess the charism of community formation and leadership, there will be no objection to their Eucharistic presidency. The charisms of all will be recognised, as in the Pauline churches. If one charism stands out above all others, as needed by Christianity today, it is prophecy, to light our path, as in the early Church. I am confident that when John Collins' recent explorations of the meaning of *diakonia* are spread abroad, and the charism-bearer is seen as the messenger of God, not as a mere servant, Christians will adopt more confidently their new roles.[50]

Above all, the new structures, especially the smallest unit, will be instrumental in a great outward movement to the world. Christians cannot continue to stand by while fifteen million children on this planet die of hunger and preventable disease each year. Two-thirds of the world's population go to bed hungry every night. Unjust economic structures which keep the Third World in debt to the banking moguls of the West must be addressed. In Australia, the appalling living conditions and treatment of Aborigines is another challenge. The planet is under threat as never before, its fauna and flora despoiled. Can Christians continue to watch the Creator's handiwork wantonly set upon? In the first three centuries, the Roman world was converted to Christianity by lay Christians, before the advent of priests. Rowan Ireland sees the tide of secularisation being turned back by the vibrant life of the base communities.[51] A new fire is about to flame on earth. The Kingdom Jesus preached is closer to fulfilment.

1. *ABC Television program, November 1986.*
2. *R. J. McClory, 'How Catholics Can Avoid the Priest Shortage: Move',* National Catholic Reporter, *21 September 1990, p. 14.*
3. *Quoted by John A. Coleman in 'Ministry in the 1980s', a lecture delivered at the Jesuit School of Theology, Berkeley, California, 1979, from an article in Dutch by Jan Kerkhofs.*
4. *Alex Cosgrave, 'Crisis of Ministry',* The Tablet, *20 July 1985, p. 746.*
5. *'The Age Distribution of Diocesan Priests',* L'Osservatore Romano, *1 November 1987, pp. 3–4.*
6. *Thomas Franklin O'Meara,* Theology of Ministry, *Paulist Press, New York, 1983, p. 125.*
7. *Edward Schillebeeckx, 'Catholic Understanding of Office in the Church',* Theological Studies *vol. 30, no. 4, December 1969, p. 569.*
8. *1 Corinthians 12:28.*
9. *Bernard Cooke,* Ministry to Word and Sacraments, *Fortress Press, Philadelphia, 1980, p. 538.*
10. *ibid. p. 541.*
11. *ibid. p. 542.*

12. *Hans Küng,* The Church, *Image Books, New York, 1976, p. 236.*
13. *Cooke, p. 244.*
14. *Küng, p. 237.*
15. *O'Meara, p. 76.*
16. *Küng, p. 241.*
17. *Kenan B. Osborne,* Priesthood: A History of Ordained Ministry in the Roman Catholic Church, *Paulist Press, New York, 1988, p. 193.*
18. *Edward Schillebeeckx, 'The Christian Community and its Office-Bearers' in* Concilium 133: Right of the Community to a Priest, *1980, eds E. Schillebeeckx & J.-B. Metz; M. Lefébure, Eng. language edition, T. T. Clark Ltd., Edinburgh; Seabury Press, N.Y. p. 95.*
19. *David N. Power,* Gifts That Differ: Lay Ministries Established and Unestablished, *Pueblo Publishing, New York, 1980, p. 70.*
20. *ibid. p. 76.*
21. *ibid. p. 79.*
22. *ibid. p. 84.*
23. *Joseph Jungmann,* The Mass of the Roman Rite, *rev. & abridged edn, Burn & Oates, London, 1959, p. 63.*
24. *ibid. p. 64.*
25. *Edward Schillebeeckx,* Ministry: Leadership in the Community of Jesus Christ, *Crossroad, New York, 1980, pp. 57–8.*
26. *ibid. p. 52.*
27. *Joseph M. Powers, 'Eucharist: Symbol of Freedom and Community', in* Christian Spirit in the United States: Independence and Interdependence, *eds A. Eigo & Silvio E. Fittipaldi, Villanova University Press, Villanova, 1978, pp. 187–8.*
28. *Tad W. Guzie,* Jesus and the Eucharist, *Paulist Press, New York, 1974, p. 63.*
29. *Jungmann, p. 65.*
30. *ibid. p. 88.*
31. *Osborne, p. 234.*
32. *Karl Rahner,* The Shape of the Church to Come, *Crossroad, New York, 1983, p. 108.*
33. *Gustavo Gutierrez, 'The Irruption of the Poor in Latin America and the Christian Communities of the Common People', in* The Challenge of Basic Communities, *eds S. Torres and J. Eagleson, Orbis Books, New York, 1982, p. 107.*
34. *Jon Sobrino, 'The Witness of the Church in Latin America', in ibid. p. 169.*
35. *Jose Marins,* Back to the Future Workshop, *Paulian Association, Sydney, 21–23 July 1990.*
36. *Margaret and Ian Fraser,* Wind and Fire, *Basic Communities Resource Centre, SEC, Dunblane, Scotland, 1986.*
37. *Edward Schillebeeckx, 'The Christian Community and its Office-Bearers', p. 95.*
38. *Karl Rahner,* The Shape of the Church to Come, *p. 110.*
39. *Leonardo Boff,* Ecclesiogenesis: The Base Communities Reinvent the Church, *Collins, London 1986, pp. 70–1.*
40. *ibid. pp. 1–2.*
41. *Edward Schillebeeckx, 'The Christian Community and its Office-Bearers', p. 127.*
42. *Karl Rahner,* Concern for the Church: Theological Investigations XX, *Crossroad, New York, 1981, p. 123.*
43. *Edward Schillebeeckx, 'Catholic Understanding of Office in the Church', p. 570.*
44. *ibid. p. 568.*
45. *Edward Schillebeeckx, 'The Christian Community and its Office-Bearers', p. 121.*
46. *Patrick Granfield,* The Papacy in Transition, *Gill & Macmillan, Dublin, 1981, p. 86.*
47. *Karl Rahner,* Concern for the Church, *p. 139.*
48. *Ian M. Fraser,* Reinventing Theology as the People's Work, *3rd edn, Wild Goose Publications, Glasgow, 1988, prologue.*
49. *Granfield, p. 185.*
50. *John Collins,* Diakonia: Re-interpreting the Ancient Sources, *Oxford University Press, New York, 1990.*
51. *Rowan Ireland, 'What Sort of Church? What Sort of Laity?', lecture delivered at the Australian Association for the Study of Religions Conference, Adelaide, August 1986.*

12. Hebe Kae, *The Church Triumphant*, New York, 1 ... p. 2 ...

13. *Ibid.*, p. 24 ...

14. *King*, p. XV

15. *Ibid.*, p. 76.

16. *King*, p. 212.

21. Rosaind Brooke, Patrick, A *Reform* ... Authority (Aggiornamento in the Roman Catholic Church), Cambridge Mass 1992, pp. 134.

... Leonard Swidler, The Consistory Synagogue ... Catholic Press, 191, Chapter 139 Right of the Community in the Church, 19 ... ...

... Victoria Reyner Otho ... F ... Gotti ... Philadelphia, 19 ... , ...

29 ... Hans Küng, *Infallible?* ... Cho ... Philadelphia Press, 19 ... , pp. ...

... Hans Küng, *Infallible?* ... by Edward Quinn, Garden City, N.Y., Double ...

... *Ibid.*, Chapter Fantasy... by Vaticanum II the papal infallibility ...

... *Ibid.*, pp. ...

20 *Ibid.*, p. 76.

21 *Ibid.*, p. 77.

22 *Ibid.*, p. 84.

23 Joseph Ratzinger, *The Ratzinger Report on the State of the Catholic Church*, trans. ... Fowler, 198 ... p. 63.

24 *Ibid.*, p. 64.

25 Edward Schillebeeckx, *Ministry, Leadership in the Community of Jesus Christ*, trans. ... New York, 1981, p. ...

26 *Ibid.*, p. 52.

27 John Mahoney, *The Making of Moral Theology, A Study of the Roman Catholic Tradition*, Oxford, 1987.

28 Gerald A. Arbuckle, *Strategies for Growth in Religious Life*, New York, 1987, p. ...

29 *Ibid.*, p. 81.

30 *Ibid.*, p. 88.

31 *Ibid.*, p. 22.

42 Karl Rahner, *The Shape of the Church to Come*, ... trans. ... New York, 1974, p. 108.

43 *Custom in Canon Law* ...

51 *Ibid.*, pp. ...

52 ...

The Twelve
and the Discipleship
of Equals

For Patricia Brennan in deep appreciation for her vision

Elisabeth
Schüssler Fiorenza

he Problem

Against the understanding of the early Christian movement as a discipleship of equals[1] it is often argued that Jesus chose and commissioned twelve men to be the apostolic leaders of the early Church. The institution of the twelve apostles—so the argument goes— proves that the hierarchically ordered apostolic ministry stood above the equality of all believers[2] in the very beginnings of the Church. Since the twelve apostles were, according to the gospels, without exception men, it is concluded that women could not have had equal access to leadership functions either in the Jesus movement or in the early Christian missionary movement. Therefore, the notion of a 'discipleship of equals' is declared to be a feminist projection back into the first century which has no support in our source texts.

Such an argument rests, however, on several faulty assumptions. It overlooks the understandings of the early Christian movement that I have conceptualised as a 'discipleship of equals', as 'equality in the spirit', as 'equality from below', or as *ekklesia*, i.e. the democratic decision-making assembly of equals as counter-terms to the structures of domination and exclusion which are institutionalised in Graeco-Roman patriarchy.[3]

Moreover, the argument against the reconstruction of early Christianity as a 'discipleship of equals' seems to imply that social equality expressed in decentralised, horizontal social structures does not admit of leadership functions. However, studies of Hellenistic and Jewish—as well as early Christian— missionary propaganda have shown that although the vast majority of religions in the Graeco-Roman world "did not develop centralised hierarchical structures", they were not without missionary leadership.[4]

In addition, this objection presupposes not only that the maleness of the Twelve is constitutive for their early Christian function but also that this function was that of apostolic leadership in the early Christian churches. Thus this objection seems to assume that the circle of the Twelve was identical with the wider circle of apostles, as well as with the wider circle of disciples.

Finally, this objection to the understanding of the early Christian movements as a 'discipleship of equals' reads the Gospels in a positivist fashion as an accurate description of the events and agents in early Christian beginnings. However, on methodological grounds, such an assumption must be judged as outdated and ideological.[5] It overlooks the rhetorical character of the Gospels as theological responses to particular historical ecclesial situations.

The Twelve and the Apostles

Popular and ecclesiastical understandings[6] generally assume that the terms 'apostles' and the 'Twelve' are coextensive categories as if both terms connote the very same historical circle and the same disciples' functions. Yet this assumption goes against the technical evidence of the scholarly consensus that the apostles and the Twelve were different circles in early Christianity, which only in the course of time were identified with each other.[7] Originally the word 'apostle' describes the function of a commissioned messenger. In the Pauline correspondence it designates a missionary sent by the Resurrected One. Clearly, the title is not restricted to the group of the 'Twelve, since Paul would not then qualify as an apostle. Insofar as not every apostle was a member of the Twelve, the term apostle seems to connote originally an independent and more comprehensive circle of leadership in the early Church.

Only at a later stage of the tradition are the twelve identified with the apostles (cf. Mark 6:30; Matthew 10:2; Revelation 21:14), an identification that is especially characteristic of the Lukan work. However, it remains debated at what point of the tradition the Twelve were also understood as apostles. Paul and Barnabas, for instance, are known as apostles in early Christianity (cf. Acts 14:4,14), but they definitely did not belong to the circle of the Twelve.

Moreover, our sources indicate that the circle of the Twelve as a circle independent of the apostles is firmly rooted in the tradition. They are already traditional figures of the past

111

towards the end of the first century (cf. Revelation 21:14).[8] The terms used are 'the Twelve', 'The twelve disciples', the 'twelve apostles' and 'the Eleven'. It is astonishing that direct references to the Twelve are rare in the Pauline writings (one in a traditional formula) and the Johannine literature (four) and completely absent in the Catholic and Pastoral Epistles. In the Pastorals it is Paul who has become the apostle par excellence.

Finally, although the four Gospel accounts about the Twelve (Mark 3:16-19; Matthew 10:2-4; Luke 6:12-16; Acts 1:13) differ,[9] they agree in listing only male names. Therefore, popular understanding assumes that the maleness of the Twelve is essential for their function and mission. One must therefore ask whether it is essential for the Twelve's mission and historical significance that they are males and whether masculinity is integral to their function.

Do the early traditions about the Twelve elaborate the male gender of the Twelve and do they reflect on it? Moreover, is the function and mission of the Twelve, according to our sources, continued in the structure and leadership of the early Church? Did the Twelve have successors, and if so did they have to be male? In other words, do we find any evidence in early Christian sources for the assumption that biological maleness and masculine gender were intrinsic to the function and mission of the Twelve and therefore must remain intrinsic to the apostolic office of the Church?

The Earliest Traditions about the Twelve

First Corinthians 15:5 and the Jesus saying in Matthew 19:28 (cf. Luke 22:30), are the two oldest source-texts that refer to the Twelve. In 1 Corinthians 15:3-5, Paul quotes a tradition which he has already received.[10] This pre-Pauline tradition maintains that the Resurrected One appeared first to Cephas and then to the Twelve. The text refers to the Twelve as a fixed and well-known group. Since it does not speak of Peter and the Eleven, the text does not reflect the defection of Judas as the resurrection narratives of the Gospels do when they consistently refer to the Eleven. Furthermore, the traditional formula in 1 Corinthians 15:3-5 does not indicate whether the group of the Twelve existed already before Easter as a definite circle of disciples in the ministry of Jesus, or whether it was constituted by the resurrection appearances and commission of the Risen One.

Paul's account parallels the statement in 1 Corinthians 15:5 with the statement in 15:7, which refers to the appearance of the Risen One to James and then to "all the apostles". It is not clear whether it was Paul who articulated the parallel statements of 1 Corinthians 15:5 and 15:7 or whether he had already found this parallel in his tradition.[11]

In any case, the present text appears to combine two different traditions and to speak of two different groups, namely, the Twelve and the apostles. As Peter stands out among the Twelve, so does James among the apostles. However, neither the pre-Pauline tradition nor the Pauline text reflect upon the gender of the Twelve nor on that of the apostles.

The very old saying, Matthew 19:28 (parallel text, Luke 22:30), has a quite different form and setting in Matthew and Luke. Even though the Matthean and Lukan form of the saying are redactional,[12] the contrast between present sufferings and future glory is common to both. In its original form the saying is an eschatological promise to the disciples who have followed Jesus. This Q-logion,[13] in its Matthean form, explicitly interprets the number twelve. When in the new world the Human One (*hyios tou anthropou*) will be revealed in all splendor and glory, the followers of Jesus also will sit "on twelve thrones to judge [or rule] the twelve tribes of Israel" (Matthew 19:28).

The text clearly does not underline the historical existence of a group of twelve men, but the function which the disciples of Jesus would have for Israel in the eschatological future. The faithful disciples will share with Jesus in the exercise of authority and power when the *basileia* is established. Since at the time of Jesus only two and a half tribes still existed, the number twelve is clearly symbolic. The circle of the Twelve thus has an eschatological-symbolic function.

The number twelve refers back to the ancient constitution of Israel consisting of twelve tribes, as well as forward to the eschatological restitution of Israel. The 'maleness' of the twelve disciples is not explicitly mentioned in this Q-logion. It could be inferred that the Twelve must be male since the text seems to refer to and to symbolise the ancient tribal constitution of Israel, which in its religious and political leadership was patriarchal.[14] Yet the logion does not refer to the historical constitution of Israel but rather points to Israel's eschatological future. It does not refer to the Church in the interim time but to the eschatological restitution of the people of Israel. This Q-saying does not postulate a historical continuum between Jesus, the Twelve, and the Church, but establishes a symbolic coherence between Jesus, the Twelve, and the eschatological reconstitution of the twelve tribes of Israel.

Revelation 21:14 also indicates that the signifying function of the Twelve is eschatological-symbolic rather than historical-masculine. According to this text the eschatological city, the New Jerusalem, is patterned after the twelve tribes of Israel: "The city walls stood on twelve foundation stones, each one of which bore the name of one of the twelve apostles of the Lamb." Here the twelve apostles are not said to be the foundation of the Church but of the New Jerusalem, which clear is an eschatological reality.[15]

Finally, one cannot argue that this Q-saying was formulated only late in the ministry of Jesus and therefore did not have a great impact on the mission and the function of the Twelve. Since the present position of the saying in Matthew and Luke is editorial, we no longer know when this saying was formulated. From a tradition-historical point of view, it could have been spoken by the historical Jesus since it reflects the heart of his preaching to and concern for the renewal of his own people (Matthew 10:5-6). Thus it seems justified to conclude:

> *The Twelve exemplified the awakening of Israel and its gathering in the eschatological salvific community, something beginning then through Jesus. They exemplified this gathering simply through the fact that they were created as twelve but they also exemplified it through being sent out to all of Israel.*[16]

The Markan Understanding of the Twelve

According to the Gospel of Mark the Twelve are likewise sent

114

to the messianic people of God, Israel, in order to carry on Jesus' ministry and work. The two main passages cited for the historical mission of the Twelve are Mark 3:13-19 and 6:6b-13. Most scholars suggest that these texts were formulated by the Markan redaction.[17] They therefore do not reflect the earliest tradition but spell out Mark's theological understanding of the Twelve. These Markan texts stress that the specific power and authority given to the Twelve is that of exorcism.[18] Mark 3:14 mentions their mission to preach but underlines that power is given to them to cast out demons. According to the commissioning scene in Mark 6:6b-13, they are neither explicitly authorised (v. 7b) nor commissioned (vv. 8-10) to preach. Their preaching is not mentioned in the concluding statement of verse 12. But the following verse 13, stresses again the power of the Twelve to heal and to cast out demons. A careful reading of the text indicates that in Mark's view the Twelve are primarily sent, and have received the power of exorcism and healing, while Jesus is the one who proclaims the gospel of the *basileia* (1:14f).[19]

It should be noted that Mark's theological emphasis on the empowerment of the Twelve to cast out demons and to heal is completely neglected by the theological articulation of 'apostolic succession'. Moreover, according to Mark, not only the twelve apostles preach (*keryssein*), but also John the Baptist (1:4, 7) and those who are healed (1:45; 5:20) or who are witnesses of healing (7:36), as well as the post-Easter community as a whole (13:10; 14:9). Further, the preaching activity of the Twelve addresses Israel. Since, in distinction to Matthew (28:16-20), Mark does not know of a post-Easter commissioning of the Twelve to universal mission, it could be inferred that Mark intends to limit the preaching of the Twelve to Galilee.

Finally, Mark 3:13-19 and 6:6b-13 do not stress that the Twelve have *to be* like Jesus but demand that, as the disciples of Jesus, the Twelve have *to do* what Jesus did. In Mark's view, Jesus is the teacher par excellence who has great authority over demons and the power to heal. Jesus' power is demonstrated by exorcisms and healing-miracles. If Mark understands the Twelve and all the other disciples to be the functional

115

successors of Jesus, then it is not their maleness but their preaching, exorcising and healing power that continues Jesus' mission.

Important too is the fact that Mark does not differentiate between but rather identifies the Twelve and the disciples.[20] A comparison of Mark 11:11 with 11:14, and Mark 14:12,14 with 14:17 speaks for the overlapping of both groups. Mark 4:10 does not provide a sufficient textual basis for a clear-cut distinction between the Twelve and the disciples, since such a separation cannot be maintained for the subsequent passages (Mark 6:35-44; 7:17; 9:28, 10:10). Insofar as Mark does not stress the apostolic character of the Twelve, even though he is aware of it (cf. 3:14 and 6:30), he clearly is not concerned with the theological foundation of apostolic ministry. He primarily understands the Twelve as disciples and attributes to them no distinctive function and mission other than discipleship. The mission of the Twelve to do what Jesus did is therefore, according to Mark, not restricted to the Twelve but is a mission given to all disciples.

The second part of the Gospel therefore stresses again and again that the disciples have to suffer the same consequences that Jesus had to suffer for his preaching and mission. Just as the way of Jesus led to suffering and death, so does the way of the true disciple. Connected with each passion prediction are statements stressing that no possibility of discipleship exists apart from taking upon oneself its consequence of suffering. Yet, again and again, the Twelve with their leading spokesman, Peter, show that they do not understand and even reject Jesus' insistence on suffering discipleship.

The twelve disciples who were called "to be with his companions" (Mark 3:14), desert Jesus in the hour of his suffering (14:50), and Peter denies him three times (14:66-72). They are not found under the cross of Jesus, nor at his burial, and it remains unclear whether they receive the message of the Resurrection (Mark 16:7-8). In marked contrast to the twelve disciples, the women disciples who have followed Jesus from Galilee to Jerusalem (cf. 15:40f) have remained faithful until the end.

Not the Twelve, but the women disciples prove to be the true disciples of Jesus in Mark. The women not only accompany

116

Jesus on his way to suffering and death but they also *do* what he had come to do, namely, to serve (*diakonein*, cf. 10:42–5 and 15:41). While the twelve disciples are unable to understand and to accept Jesus' teaching that he must suffer, it is a woman who shows such perception and acts accordingly (14:3–9). In Mark her action is the immediate cause for the betrayal of Jesus by one of the Twelve (14:10f). This contrast between the Twelve and the women disciples would suggest that in Mark's church the apostolic women were considered to have been the exemplary disciples of Jesus who had their place among the leaders of the Jesus movement in Palestine.[21] In Mark's theological perspective, the women disciples are the functional successors of Jesus and they continue Jesus' mission and ministry in the 'New Family' of God. Far from being the exemplars of apostolic discipleship, the Twelve are the negative blueprint of right discipleship.

Luke's Theological Accentuation

Since Luke-Acts has formed our theological understanding and historical imagination of early Christian beginnings, its identification of the Twelve with the apostles has greatly influenced Christian theological and historical self-understanding. Nevertheless, the Lukan redaction still views the circle of the Twelve as belonging to the time of Jesus and to the very beginnings of the Christian movement. The Twelve's legitimisation is rooted in their companionship with Jesus and in their witness to the Resurrection. They have special eschatological (Q) and historical (Mark) functions *vis-à-vis* Israel.

It is debatable whether Acts 1:21ff[22] makes maleness explicitly a precondition for replacing a member of the Twelve. According to Luke the position of Judas can be taken "Out of the men (*aner*) who have been with us the whole time that the Lord Jesus was living with us, from the time John was baptising until the day when he was taken up from us". Thus, according to Luke-Acts only one of the original disciples of Jesus who were, together with the Eleven, witnesses to the Resurrection could replace Judas, who was one of the Twelve. However, it is not clear whether *aner* is used in 1:21 in a grammatically generic or in a gender specific masculine sense, since Acts often uses the address 'men, brothers' (1:16; 23:29; 2:37; 7:2; 13:15; 13:26,38; 15:7,13; 22:1,6; 28:17) in a grammatically generic-inclusive sense for addressing the whole community, even when women are present (cf. 1:14 and 1:16).

It could, however, also be argued to the contrary that because of his theological understanding of the Twelve, Luke maintains that only one of the *male* followers of Jesus is eligible to become one of the Twelve, since Luke 8:1-3 clearly distinguishes between the women disciples of Jesus and the Twelve. Differing from its Markan source, the Gospel of Luke has the women disciples serve Jesus *and* the Twelve. It qualifies their *diakonein* insofar as it specifies that the women disciples served them, i.e. Jesus and the Twelve, with their possessions. Just as wealthy women provided patronage for Jewish missionary endeavours, so, according to Luke, wealthy Christian women support the ministry of Jesus and of the twelve apostles. Luke then seems to limit the leadership role of women in the Christian missionary movement to that of benefactors.[23]

However, Luke-Acts precludes the notion that the Twelve could have appointed a line of successors, since Luke's theological perspective assigns only a very limited function to the twelve apostles. The Twelve are mentioned for the last time in Acts 6:2ff, and they disappear altogether after chapter 15. It is, moreover, curious that most passages in Acts speak only of the work of one of them, Peter. Luke-Acts does not characterise the Twelve as missionaries, and there is little evidence in Acts that they were at all active outside Jerusalem. In Acts the apostle par excellence is Paul, who clearly was not one of the Twelve.

Luke knows likewise that the Twelve were not the official local ministers of the Jerusalem church or any other church. According to Paul and Acts, the leadership of the Jerusalem church was in the hands of James, the brother of the Lord, who was not one of the Twelve. Moreover, the Twelve as a group were not replaced when they died (cf. Acts 12:2). The twelve apostles had no successors. Thus it is evident that Luke knows only of a very limited function for the Twelve in the origins of the Christian movements. Their significance appears

118

to be limited to the very beginnings of the Church and to its relationship to the chosen people of Israel.

Following Mark, Luke seems to historicise / the eschatological-symbolic function *vis-à-vis* Israel which the Twelve had in his tradition. He limits their activity to the mission within Israel. After the gentile mission is under way, the Twelve disappear from the historical scene. The elders and bishops in Acts are not understood as successors of the Twelve. They are either appointed by Paul and Barnabas (14:23) or directly called by the Holy Spirit (20:28).

In conclusion, it needs to be stressed that according to Luke-Acts the historical and symbolic function of the Twelve was not continued in the ministries of the Church. Neither their eschatological-symbolic and historical-missionary function *vis-à-vis* Israel nor their function as eyewitnesses of the ministry and resurrection of Jesus is constitutive for the ministry of the Church. If Luke should have required that the replacement of Judas must be a male follower of the historical Jesus, then this does not say anything about maleness as an essential requirement for the ordained priesthood or episcopacy in the Church, since Luke does not envision any 'apostolic succession' of the Twelve. The theological problem at hand is then whether the theological construct of 'apostolic succession' can be maintained today in view of the historical recognition that the twelve apostles had no successors.

The historical-theological issue at stake is therefore not whether women can be appointed as successors of the apostles if Jesus did not call any woman disciple to be a member of the circle of Twelve. Rather the theological issue at hand is whether the discipleship of equals will be realised by the *ekklesia*, the democratic assembly of *all* citizens in the Church. As long as such a vision of the *ekklesia of women* has not become a reality, apostolic calling engages women and men in the struggle for the transformation of the patriarchal Church into the discipleship community of equals.

This is a revised form of a French version which has appeared in *Foi et Vie* (Cahier Biblique 28) vol. LXXXVIII, 1989, pp. 13–24.

1. *For this expression see my book,* In Memory of Her: A Feminist Theological Reconstruction of Christian Origins, *Crossroad, New York, 1983; cf. also R.L. Sider, 'Toward a Biblical Perspective on Equality',* Interpretation, *vol. XLIII, 1989, pp. 156–69.*

2. *For such an argument see L. W. Countryman, 'Christian Equality and the Early Catholic Episcopate',* Anglican Theological Review, *vol. 63, 1981, p. 115.*

3. *See my article, 'Die Anfänge von Kirche, Amt, und Priestertum in feministisch-theologischer Sicht', in P. Hoffman,* Priesterkirche, Theologie der Zeit, *vol. 3, Patmos, Düsseldorf, 1987, pp. 62–95.*

4. *Cf. the epilogue in D. Georgi,* The Opponents of Paul in Second Corinthians, *Fortress Press, Philadelphia, 1986, p. 362 and E. Schüssler Fiorenza, ed.,* Aspects of Religious Propaganda in Judaism and Early Christianity, *Notre Dame University Press, Notre Dame, 1976.*

5. *For a discussion of such a positivist approach see my 'Text and Reality—Reality as Text: the Problem of a Feminist Historical and Social Reconstruction Based on Texts',* Studia Theologica, *vol. 43, 1989, pp. 19–34 and my Society of Biblical Literature presidential address, 'The Ethics of Interpretation',* Journal of Biblical Literature, *vol. 107, 1988, pp.3–17.*

6. *See my articles, 'The Twelve' and 'The Apostleship of Women in Early Christianity', in L. and A. Swidler, eds,* Women Priests: A Catholic Commentary on the Vatican Declaration, *Paulist Press, New York, 1977, pp. 114–22 and 135–40; J. A. Kirk, 'Apostleship since Rengstorf',* New Testament Studies, *vol. 21, 1974/75, p. 260 ff; Andrew C. Clark, 'Apostleship: Evidence from the New Testament and Early Christian Literature',* Vox Evangelica *vol. XIX, 1989, pp. 49–82.*

7. *For a general discussion of the problem cf. B. Rigaux, 'The Twelve Apostles',* Concilium, *vol. 34, 1968, pp. 5–15; 'Die "Zwölf" in Geschichte und Kerygma', in Ristow-Matthiae, ed.,* Der Historische Jesus und der kerygmatische Christus, *2nd ed., Berlin, 1961, pp. 468–86; G. Klein,* Die Zwölf Apostel: Ursprung und Gehalt einer Idee, Forschungen zur Religion und Literatur des Alten und Neuen Testaments, *vol. 59, Vandenhoeck & Ruprecht, Gottingen, 1961; J. Roloff,* Apostolat—Verkündigung—Kirche, *Mohn, Gütersloh, 1965; R. Schnackenburg, 'Apostolicity: The Present Position of Studies',* One in Christ, *vol. 6, 1970, pp. 243–73; V. Taylor,* The Gospel According to St Mark, *2nd ed., Macmillan, London, 1966, pp. 619–27; A Vögtle in* Lexikon für Theologie und Kirche, *Vol. IX, 2nd ed., Herder, Frieburg, 1966, pp. 1443ff; H. D. Betz,* Galatians, Hermeneia, *Fortress, Philadelphia, 1979 p. 74f (Excursus: Apostle).*

8. *See my book,* Priester für Gott: Studien zum Herrschafts- und Priestermotiv in der Apokalypse, *Aschendorff, Münster, 1972.*

9. *For a discussion of the text and of the secondary literature see Joseph A. Fitzmyer,* The Gospel According to Luke, *Anchor Bible 28AB, Doubleday, Garden City, 1985, pp. 613–21.*

10. *For extensive bibliographic information cf. H. Conzelmann,* I Corinthians, Hermeneia, *Fortress, Philadelphia, 1975, pp. 251–4.*

11. *For an extensive discussion and literature cf. H. Merklein,* Das kirchliche Amt nach dem Epheserbrief, *Studia Antoniana, Kösel, München, 1973, pp. 273–8.*

12. *For a discussion of the original Q-form and the Matthean and Lukan redaction see Fitzmyer, pp. 1413ff.*

13. *Q is used to designate the source of the material that is common to Matthew and Luke but is not found in Mark. Since the material is almost wholly teaching material Q is often called 'Sayings-source' or Logia source.*

14. *However, Christian feminists must learn to read such information in an anti-patriarchal fashion rather than perpetuate scholarly anti-Jewish readings. See Judith Plaskow,* Standing Again at Sinai: Judaism from a Feminist Perspective, *Harper & Row, New York, 1990.*

15. *For a comprehensive interpretation of Revelation see my book,* Revelation: Vision of a Just World, *Fortress, Minneapolis, 1991.*

16. *G. Lohfink,* Jesus and Community: The Social Dimension of Christian Faith, *Fortress, Philadelphia, 1984, p. 10. See also Ulrich Luz,* Das Evangelium nach Matthäus II, *Benzinger/Neukirchener Verlag, Zürich, 1990, pp. 74–161.*

17. *Cf. J. Coutts, 'The Authority of Jesus and the Twelve in St Mark's Gospel',* Journal of Theological Studies, *vol. 8, 1957, pp. 111–18; K. G. Reploh,* Markus—Lehrer der

Gemeinde, *Stuttgarter biblische Monagraphien*, vol. 9. *Katholisches Bibelwerk*, Stuttgart, 1969, pp. 43–58; K. Stock, Boten aus dem Mit-Ihm-Sein: Das Verhältnis zwischen Jesus und den Zwölf nach Markus, *Analecta Biblica*, vol. 70, *Biblical Institute Press*, Rome, 1975; G. Schmahl, 'Die Berufung der Zwölf im Markusevangelium', Trierer theologische Zeitschrift, vol. 81, 1972, pp. 203–313; R. Pesch, Das Markusevangelium: 1: Teil, *Herders theologischer Kommentar zum Neuen Testament*, II/ 1, Herder, Freiburg, 1976, pp. 202–9, 325–32 (literature).

18. *Cf. K. Kertelge, 'Die Funktion der "Zwölf" im Markusevangelium', Trierer theologische Zeitschrift, vol. 78, 1969, pp. 193–206.

19. *Cf. Ched Myers, Binding the Strong Man: A Political Reading of Mark's Story of Jesus, Orbis Books, Maryknoll, 1988, p. 164, who stresses the political dimension of this symbolic act: Jesus forms a "kind of vanguard 'revolutionary committee' ".

20. *Against K. Stock, who ascribes to the Twelve a special function, namely to represent Jesus and to continue his work. Cf., however, K. G. Reploh, pp. 47f, who maintains that the Twelve are included among the disciples. They have no special function distinctive from the disciples but they are the origin and beginning of the whole Church. See also U. Luz, who warns not to restrict the commissioning of the twelve disciples to a limited historical circle and thereby to excuse the* ekklesia *from practicing the ethos of discipleship.*

21. *Cf. P. J. Achtemeier, Mark, Proclamation Commentary, Fortress, Philadelphia, 1975, pp. 92–100.

22. *For Acts 1:15–26 cf. E. Haenchen, The Acts of the Apostles, Westminster, Philadelphia, 1971, pp. 157–65 (literature).

23 *For a different interpretation cf. H. Conzelmann, The Theology of Saint Luke, Faber & Faber, London, 1961, p. 47 n. 1: "Features from the primitive community have naturally been projected back. Just as the male followers are turned into apostles, so the female followers are turned into deaconesses (v. 3)." F. W. Danker, Jesus and the New Age, rev. ed., Fortress, Philadelphia, 1988, p. 172f, on the other hand stresses that the women are to "be included within the class of benefactors that was so esteemed in Mediterranean society... ", but he does not reflect on the Lukan redactional tendencies that determine this inclusion. For a feminist analysis of such tendencies cf. my book, But She Said, Beacon Press, Boston, 1992.*

A Theological Seminary's Bold Venture:

Teaching Feminist Liberation Theology

Alison M. Cheek

or some years now I have been involved as a learner-teacher and teacher-learner in the field of feminist liberation theology and ministry at the Episcopal Divinity School in Cambridge, Massachusetts, in the USA. The invitation to contribute an article to the *festschrift* honouring Patricia Brennan began a process of reflection for me on my current commitment as Director of Feminist Liberation Theology Studies at EDS.[1] Feminist liberation theology pays attention to context and to the particularities within a context. EDS is a particular school, with a particular history, in a particular geographical area of the world. Yet the issues which rise up to meet me as I reflect on its struggles to live justly as a Christian theological seminary in today's pluralistic world are not unrelated to the struggles for justice of women and men in my own home country of Australia.[2]

In this article I begin to name some of the areas of struggle in my own context in the hope that there will be connections for Australian readers and that the dialogue amongst us all will be served. In particular I reflect on some of the dynamics involved in a setting for theological education which is in some degree multicultural.

I came to the EDS as a white, middle-strata, heterosexual woman, a widow, a mother and grandmother, a psychotherapist and a Christian priest, and out of this context began to work on a Doctor of Ministry degree in feminist liberation theology. It was only gradually that I became aware of the implications of my social location, and of the social location of the school, and began to analyse these implications in the light of the Christian's call to the work of justice.

My initial awareness was the pressing need to rethink my theology. I knew that I had received a good basic theological education at the Virginia Theological Seminary in the 1960s, but since that time not only had much new discourse taken place, particularly in the areas of liberation theology and feminist theology, but it was apparent to me that my own life experience had outstripped the usefulness of my inherited theology. The words and concepts no longer made as much sense to me as once they had. The Doctor of Ministry degree, I thought, would provide a framework and impetus to do the needed work.

I came into the program from working on the margins of the Church. I had been co-director with Joan Bauer of an experimental project for women who were feeling the oppressiveness of Church and synagogue, and for those who had left institutional religion yet were seeking authentic ways in which to express their spirituality. The project was named Well Woman, drawing on the biblical story of the woman at the well in John's Gospel and a play on the word 'well' in relation to wholeness and health. While very successful with the constituency, the Well Woman project had foundered over structural and financial issues.

In the feminist liberation theology Doctor of Ministry program every student must successfully complete eight courses and a thesis/project. The thesis/project is a dissertation which embodies both a theoretical and an applied ministry component. My first thought for a thesis/project was to take my experience at Well Woman and analyse the issues involved in its rise and fall, so that women would not have to reinvent the wheel every time they embarked on a similar endeavour.

However, the experience proved to be too close and raw and I turned to another interest—the ways in which imagination may be used in breaking open old thought forms and opening up the possibility of new ways of thinking. In relation to this interest I embarked on a thesis/project which dealt with Bible study as consciousness raising, using imagination as an entry point and drawing on the tools provided by Elisabeth Schüssler Fiorenza in her fourfold hermeneutical model.[3]

Meanwhile my own consciousness raising proceeded. I became aware of the varieties of feminist theologies, their interweaving and distinctiveness. I chose to pursue feminist liberation theology. This meant that I had to become much more keenly sensitised to the particularities of persons in terms of race, class, ethnic community, sexual orientation, economic and cultural imperialism and exploitation, as well as in terms of gender. I had to learn the degree to which these differences do not simply give rise to personal problems to be overcome in individual relating but carry within them deep, pervasive, systemic oppressions which our dominant white culture holds in place. I had to learn to do a power analysis of these structures and to keep asking questions:

In whose interests is this custom?
Whom does this etiquette serve?
Who benefits by this norm?
Who is protected by this law?
Who is being silenced?
Who is being marginalised?
Whose reality is being trivialised?
Whose life is being forfeited?

Many white middle- and upper-class women come to a feminist consciousness through a growing awareness of gender oppression. The first reaction of a raised consciousness to the pervasive sexism in every culture is to struggle for equal rights. Often, an unexamined assumption behind this struggle is that women stand on an equal footing in their efforts to achieve equality. It is sometimes hard for white women in this culture to understand and acknowledge their privilege in relation to people of colour, both women and men, and to analyse the power differential amongst women on account of class, sexual orientation, country of origin, etc. It is difficult to name oneself as an *oppressor* by virtue of white privilege as well as *oppressed* by gender domination.

I came to EDS keenly aware of gender oppression, of the physical and psychic injuries suffered by women in a sexist and heterosexist society, and aware of its systemic nature from my own experiences of struggle within the institution of the Christian Church. Nevertheless, my history was such that I was much closer to an understanding of feminism as equal-rights feminism, integrally related to a theology of the baptised as a discipleship of equals, than to an understanding of a critical theology of liberation. I had grown up in Australia in an era when eighty per cent of the population was of British extraction, in a geographical area where I seldom even saw an Aboriginal person. My life in the United States had largely been lived out in white suburbs. I had a very limited appreciation of the daily reality of people of colour or of the structure of racism, even though I marched and worked for civil rights.

My slowly rising consciousness impelled me to take action for women's full participation and inclusion in every aspect of the life of the Episcopal Church, but I did not really ask myself why I wanted to be ordained in such an hierarchical and elitist structure. Clericalism was another 'ism' I had not fully examined. I now think one should seek ordination only if one is committed to disentangling and changing oppressive structures in both Church and society; only if one is willing, as the book of Acts says, to "turn the world upside down". This reflects a shift for me from equal-rights feminism to feminist liberation.

When I use the word 'feminist' I am not using it in terms of gender dualism. 'Feminist' is not the opposite of 'masculinist' in feminist liberation theology; it is a political oppositional term to patriarchy. Patriarchy is not the domination of all women by all men, but rather a political and social *system* in which there is an interrelated hierarchy of dominations and subordinations in regard to economic status, race and gender. 'Feminist' in this context is a term meant to convey a true and equal inclusiveness, not the domination and exploitation of one sex by another, one race by another, one class by another, one country by another. Therefore the term feminist envisages a radical shift in mind-set and in structural systems. Feminist liberation theology is not solely an academic discipline but a movement for change.

At EDS change takes place in understanding, commitment and policy—through interchanges in the classroom, in student colloquia, in committees, in the chapel (particularly through the impact of preaching) and in the common life of the school community. It comes hard. The process is slow and difficult.

When I entered the Doctor of Ministry program in feminist liberation theology, all of the students were white except for one from an Asian country. In our colloquium this student battled against language barriers to convey to us her experience and articulate her reality. Although the class listened I don't believe it was possible for us really to hear. It took several students of colour in the succeeding years of the class to provide

127

a critical mass; to provide enough voices to begin to make a dent in our understanding of the difference difference makes. Not only do these women have to convey to us that our reality is not their reality, but they also have to struggle against being lumped together as 'women of colour' when they actually come from quite disparate cultures and contexts.

Feminist liberation theology resists taking the experience and thinking of one group, the dominant group in theology and in the global power structure (white European and American men), universalising it, naming it 'objective'. It takes with utmost seriousness the particularities of social context and history, and the experience of marginalised and disregarded people becomes the methodological starting point. Because gender oppression is found in every culture it is easy for white middle- and upper-class women, who belong to the dominant culture in the USA, to identify with all women in ways which remain unexamined. There is a valid and vital identification, but we have to resist taking our white experience and universalising it for all women. Until privilege as well as oppression is analysed we cannot stand in solidarity with one another.

The presence of racism and classism create ongoing theological and educational problems at EDS. The miracle is that these problems are actually being addressed. In the past the school has predominantly trained men and women for the ordained ministry in the Episcopal Church, while providing an excellent academic education for those seeking higher degrees in theology and opening its doors to women and men with lay vocations. It has a fine record of commitment to justice and has taken courageous stands out of Christian faith and conviction. The Episcopal Church is largely a white middle- and upper-class church. It has counted more than a proportional share of the country's leaders and power brokers among its numbers. This is the social location within which EDS exists.

In recent years, through the introduction of the option of a feminist liberation theology specialisation in the Master of Arts degree and in the Doctor of Ministry degree, and through the introduction of a program in Anglicanism, Globalism and Ecumenism, the student body at EDS has diversified a little. The white middle- and upper-class students are still by far the majority, so that the school has become a microcosm of the macrocosm of the white supremacist society of the country.

The challenge to live justly in a Christian institution and the world accordingly takes on immediacy and intensity, and impacts on the way in which theology is conceived and taught. It presses us towards a paradigm shift "to change the disciplinary discourses of academic religious scholarship and of Christian theologies". Elisabeth Schüssler Fiorenza, in a presidential address to the Society of Biblical Literature and a convocation address at Harvard Divinity School, has argued:

> ... theological disciplines and institutions must explicitly reflect on their rhetorical public socio-political functions. Only when Religious and Biblical Studies decenter their stance of objectivist positivism and scientistic value-detachment and become 'engaged' scholarship, can feminist and other liberation theologies participate in defining the center of the discipline. Not the posture of value-detachment and a political objectivism but the articulation of one's social location, interpretive strategies, and theoretical frameworks are appropriate in such a rhetorical paradigm of theological studies.[4]

Such a paradigm shift is a radical one for the work of theology, although not at all radical in respect to the central tenets of Christian faith. EDS belongs to a consortium of theological schools, the Boston Technological Institute, in which all students may cross register. In most of the schools there can be found courses being taught from both of these theoretical stances, coexisting in uneasy alliance. To offer degrees, however, in feminist liberation theology is a bold position to adopt in today's theological world. Degrees in women's studies are more easily disregarded as being peripheral to biblical and theological discourse.

EDS is a school in which students may expect to find a significant number of courses being taught in an 'engaged' manner. For a woman whose primary theological degree was earned in a school where teaching was from the perspective of the male Western norm, to find herself in a class where her own particular experience is taken seriously and valued is enormously liberating. Dr Sung Min Kim, a Korean American

129

woman who is a recent graduate of our Doctor of Ministry program in feminist liberation theology, writes:

> One of the most powerful and liberating experiences I can name in encountering feminism was in being told that all of my personal experiences are legitimate sources worthy of attention for academic and political work. For more than thirty years of my life as a woman I have struggled through painful relationships, almost all of them with males who had power over me: with my authoritarian father, abusive male partners, sexual harassments and the male hierarchy of schools and church institutions. And for all those years I was ashamed that I would be spending so much energy on 'petty' personal issues when there are bigger issues of world problems that I should be dealing with like war, poverty, multinational corporations, etc. Nobody told me that they were related to each other.[5] Therefore, in my own educational work and in ministry with other people, I did not feel that it was appropriate for me to bring my personal struggles into the open... This dilemma had a tremendous effect on my work. There is nothing more liberating than having our own lives taken seriously and being affirmed in our innermost feelings.[6]

While the particularities of our lived experience are a starting point for our theological reflection, they have to be seen in relation to a larger framework. The connections must be drawn between these particularities and the structures of society. Our 'sacred stories' and our lives are challenged at EDS by the 'sacred stories' of others from a different social location. Dr Kim, who spoke about the liberating impact of a feminist methodology which begins with one's story, also has a valuable critique to offer of white feminist pedagogy.

Up to this point, the feminist liberation theology programs at EDS have attracted two men and many women. Students in these programs, in addition to their classes, work together in weekly conferences and colloquia which become in effect 'women's space'. It is in this potentially 'safe space' that the painful realities of minority students are more readily evident. For feminist liberation theology has a particular style. It is collaborative and participatory, and much of the work in it at EDS is done in small groups, where personal sharing and critique of papers takes place.

Dr Kim observes that in groups such as these, what white women bring up as their most significant experience of oppression, and what women of colour bring up as their greatest experience of oppression, have very different starting points. Generally speaking, white women usually name experiences of sexism (sexual abuses such as incest, rape, harassments, wife/child battering, sexual discrimination in jobs, schools, etc.), while women of colour name racism, cultural imperialism or US imperialism in Third World countries as the greatest form of oppression in their lives—and the presence of white women in the groups itself becomes a clear reminder of how racism is played out in the larger society.

Kim offers some reasons why white feminist pedagogy may not empower women of colour. Firstly, in most women's gatherings the settings are created by white women since they are the ones who have the power of material resources, information, personal contacts and networks. They have more institutional power than women of colour. Even when women of colour are invited to participate from the birthing stage of a program, there is no way in which they can have equal power with white women in a racist society, where it is given that white women do have more power.

Secondly, white women usually outnumber women of colour in feminist groups so that when group process entails the sharing of one's own experience, women of colour are set up to become minority voices with few people able to identify with their experiences of white supremacy and cultural imperialism. Empathy is missing here for women of colour and a feeling of powerlessness, inferiority and oppression is often experienced.

Thirdly, white women do not have to know what white supremacy is in order to survive, but have been beneficiaries of a racist system. They are often very ignorant and naive about racism. The stories of their life experiences themselves become oppressive to the women of colour and it is a source of pain and anger for them to know that their 'oppressors' do not know how they participate in the oppression of others.

When a woman of colour shares her story of how racism is

131

experienced in her life with a group of white women, she is asking for understanding, empathy, as well as recognition of privilege from white women, so that connections can be made between people that live on the two different sides of a racist society. But this does not happen easily in sharing groups, probably because white women are either too stuck in their pain and anger from their experiences of oppression, or so stuck in their feelings of guilt that it is difficult even to listen fully to the stories of women of colour. Sometimes the presence of a true listening heart is the only thing needed for the healing and empowerment of women of colour.[7]

The difficulties of truly hearing one another occur in many arenas. Students dealing with class injury, gays and lesbians dealing with heterosexist Church and world, international students dealing with cultural differences, straight white men dealing with challenge to their privilege, white women battling sexism and all students of colour dealing with racism struggle to know how to relate to each other. Nothing avails unless love and justice and power go hand in hand, and the struggle to discern the way can become hard and wearisome.

Where there is no common basis of oppression, coalition building becomes vital for the struggle towards a common goal. In a small school with limited resources groupings can be so small that no coalition formation is possible because numbers are so disproportionate. Yet even one or two people do manage to make a difference. Policies do get changed. The cost is often high.

I reflect on my own part in it all. I am often impossibly weary, yet there is no other place I want to be. What is it that nourishes me, keeps me growing, keeps me at it? How do I keep the faith? I think I keep it through a variety of traditional ways and in spite of them. But most of all it is making the connections that feeds and nourishes me. It is the kind of deep relating that my colleague, Carter Heyward, has called 'godding'.

I listen to a Korean American sister reflecting on her life, remembering her childhood. She is ten, the only person of colour in her school. A little girl in her class asks her: "Do you have any eyelashes?" She is non-plussed, yet she knows the significance of the question. She knows the child is asking her: "Are you human like me?" She tells of her method of survival growing up, longing for friends but feeling spurned because she is different, never being taken seriously. She listens to her mother's admonition that she must work hard and succeed and go to college. When she leaves the house she screens out what is going on around her, potentially so hurtful, and concentrates on the book, the assignment, the task which must be accomplished in order to succeed.

An African American sister marvels at how proactive such a stance was. She reflects on her own African American experience and speaks about the jungle stance, where one is poised to react to a sudden, unseen attack.

I listen to my sisters as a middle strata woman from the dominant culture. Their stories touch me deeply with a searing kind of pain. I realise that my response arises out of old, deep hurts of my own. It enables me to relate to what I hear with mind and spirit and body. At the same time I am aware that my own wounds were episodic and not of the same pervasive order. I begin to reflect on some of the privileges of race and class and to learn from my sisters. I have had the freedom to blurt out whatever I am thinking or feeling except in highly political situations having to do with gender discrimination and cultural norms.

Now hearing my sisters, I am impelled to strive to curb my thoughtless tongue, to listen, to observe the dynamics in one-on-one and group encounters, and to analyse the power structures and attitudes underlying them. Once again I am motivated to unearth my internalised, unconscious racism and classism, to feel the pain of each new awareness and to act vulnerably towards justice.

1. *EDS is the abbreviation used for the Episcopal Divinity School throughout this article.*
2. *'Struggle' has become for me both a theological category and the place where I live. I am reminded of a hymn that was sung at my ordination to the diaconate. The last verse reads: "The peace of God it is no peace, but strife closed in the sod. Yet let us pray for but one thing—the marvellous peace of God".* (William Alexander Percy, The Hymnal 1982 According-ing to the Use of the Episcopal Church, no. 661).
3. *This model is explicated in Elisabeth Schüssler Fiorenza,* Bread Not Stone: The Challenge of Feminist Biblical Interpretation, *Beacon Press, Boston, 1985. For an example of this use of the imagination, see Alison Cheek's 'The Epistle of Eunice to the Women in Philippi', on pp 137–9 of this volume.*

4. Elisabeth Schüssler Fiorenza, 'The Ethics of Biblical Interpretation: Decentering Biblical Scholarship', Journal of Biblical Literature, vol. 107, 1988, pp. 3–17; 'Commitment and Critical Inquiry', Harvard Theological Review, vol. 82, 1989, pp. 1–11. Quoted from 'Changing the Paradigms', in In God's Image, vol. 10, no. 1, Spring 1991.

5. Emphasis mine.

6. Sung Min Kim, Journey Towards Wholeness and Liberation Through Feminism and Wholistic Spirituality: A Korean American Immigrant Woman's Story, unpublished doctoral thesis, Episcopal Divinity School Library, Cambridge, Massachusetts.

7. ibid.

Voices

Jean Groves
Peta Sherlock
Alison Cheek
Eileen Baldry
Ali Wurm
Heather Thomson
Sr. Angela/Elaine Lindsay
Irene McCormack RSJ

A selection of writings mainly from
MOW publications, in which
women reflect on God, our
scriptures, our power and our
Eucharist.

Jean Groves

T he presence of God is like the atmosphere we breathe. You can have all you want as long as you do not try to take possession of it and hang on to it.

(Source: MOW Newsletter, Autumn 1989, p. 10.)

Peta Sherlock

L *ot's wife:*

> *Don't look back! the warning came. Which only goes to prove*
> *that this is very much the world of men in which we move.*
> *For women live by looking back, connecting now and then,*
> *unable to dislodge the past and simply start again.*
> *Women dine on past events. They savour every crumb,*
> *to feed the soul, replenish strength, and face what is to come.*
> *Past people and relationships, including Sodom's years.*
> *So you were caught by blinding light. Or blinded by your tears.*
> *And now you stand, forever salt, distilled from every tear.*
> *Your only fault, the backward glance. Alternative: unclear.*
> *And generations after you were pilloried, who'd guess*
> *another One would speak of light and value saltiness!*

And so Lot's wife revealed herself to me. Her only fault, the backward glance. A pillar of... salt! And Jesus said we are to be like salt! You can't really let go of the grief until you have looked back, and looked deeply, at what has gone before. After all, Lot's daughters, and Lot himself, may have escaped the fate of Sodom and Salt, but their subsequent actions show they were hardly freed of Sodom's influence.

I am a mere pillar of salt. I can't move, at least not very fast or far. But maybe those of us who can only glance over our shoulders can also be salt in the world.

(Source: MOW Newsletter, May 1991, p. 9.)

Alison Cheek:

The Epistle of Eunice to the Women in Philippi

*The history of women in biblical religion is hidden beneath
androcentric language and patriarchal interests. We need to
use our imaginations, as well as the tools of historical criticism,
to recover a sense of connectedness with our foresisters in the
faith. Many biblical passages prescribe what the author wishes
to see happen, rather than describe current practices. What, for
instance, was really going on in the church in Ephesus when
1 Timothy was written? That the author of 1 Timothy comes
on with the big guns must mean that there were spirited and
powerful women in the community he addresses. Their struggles
seem not unlike our struggles today. Here, then, is an exercise
in imagination:*

To Lydia and the sisters in Philippi, whose love and wisdom
and courage inspire us, from Eunice and the sisters in Ephesus,
who remain strong in the power of the Spirit and joyful in
our solidarity in the gospel. Grace and peace to you in Christ
our wisdom, manifested so freely in works of healing and deeds
of love.

The visit from Apphia and Salome with first-hand news
of you all has filled us with new hope and energy. We send
this letter back to you by their hand. They will tell you how
much we have been sustained by mutual encouragement, for
the times are hard for us here, with enemies without and
enemies within. Yet we are not downhearted. We never forget
that for freedom Christ has set us free, although there are those,
even who profess that name, who would again impose the
yoke of slavery. Nevertheless, the sisters hold firm. We meet
together daily in each other's houses for prayer and study,
and we hold you always in our thoughts and prayers.

137

There is so much going on here—so many discussions and different ideas and many an argument! We hold dear the traditions of our Sophia and her sayings preserved for us by Jesus. Indeed she is the source of all creation, the law, the Christ, our wisdom, mother, friend. We share together the traditions that have been handed down to us, and in them know our power. Yet none of it without opposition. Our 'Timothy' is getting as bad as your 'Paul'. He has produced letters which he claims authorise him to forbid our women to speak in the gatherings of the church, and to prophesy and teach. He wants women to teach only other women. There are those amongst our men who are eager to follow his instructions.

It is not only against the free and freed women that he speaks, and the slave women for whose manumission we are working, but also against the men who are still slaves. We are all to be subordinate, according to his lordship, and keep our place and speak and act submissively, as if the glorious gospel of the freedom of Christ had never been preached at all. We try to be reasonable with these brothers and gentle with their fear, but, of course, we stand firm.

It is so ridiculous. You will remember that women were responsible for starting the church here. Lois still enthralls us with tales of her grandmother and great-grandmother. I wonder if it was different in those days or if the tensions in the community were always as strong.

Indeed, our way of life is dangerous, as it is for you. We are accused of putting the whole Church at risk by our insistence on a discipleship of equals. But we keep on with our meetings and God-speak. ('Our 'Timothy' is derogating it as gossip and idle tales and silly myths.) We know, however, that it is our lifeblood and our salvation. Chloe came last month and spoke to us so powerfully in the spirit, and we had several marvellous healings. The joy and energy that flowed through our meetings were truly remarkable.

We are working very hard to buy the freedom of everyone who is still a slave in our community. I only wish the men would show as much zeal. The tide pulls against. It is a struggle, too, to keep all of our widows from feeling want. But the acts of generosity and love we witness every day testify to the bounty of our Sophia and the power of her Spirit.

May the same Spirit bind us together and pour her blessings upon your community too. We hope to send Philippa to you before long. Greetings from all of us in the name of our Sophia-God. Her peace be with you always.

(Source: MOW Newsletter, September 1987.)

Eileen Baldry:

From an Anglican consumer:

Beauty, creative art, poetry, novels and inspirations have burst through Church communities from the beginning—from Abbess Hildegard to Gerard Manley Hopkins. But it requires equally creative people to expose, not this intangible spiritual richness, but the tangible, institutional structures to criticism. Christian Churches like all societal institutions, are human constructs, organised and run, in these cases, by males. As with all institutions, those within them have the right to question whether the institutions are doing what they are supposed to be doing, whether they are helpful to living and growing for both individuals and for the community. But as the Church is one of the most conservative institutions in society, there is little encouragement to work for change and generally strong censure of those who do.

Of course, anyone can walk away from the Church if she or he doesn't like the way it operates and indeed, thousands, in particular younger women, have done just that. But there are some good arguments for hoping that many stay to debate, argue and call for change.

One reason is that the Church needs them! An organisation without worthwhile critique and dissent from within is dead. In an insightful book, *Exit, Voice and Loyalty*, Albert Hirschman (Harvard University Press, Cambridge, 1970) demonstrated that if all those who want change and progress exit from an institution instead of voicing disagreement and taking on the status quo, the institution becomes less vital, less able to respond to needs inside and outside itself. In other words, by stifling dissention or by forcing such dissenters out, an institution turns in on itself and loses vitality. The Church, which is supposed to be a living body, will become a dead body.

A second reason is that, despite its many failings, there is much in the Church worth treasuring. While it has spawned, in the name of God, some of the worst actions the world has seen, it has also been the ground from which some of the most visionary and deeply spiritual human endeavours have arisen. This must not be lost.

Thirdly, the Church in its denominational manifestations carries the potential for enormous social reform. More often than not, this potential is not realised, but now and again, through extraordinary people who take seriously the gospel's call to social action, the Church can be moved to pressure governments and the public to act justly—for instance, the stance taken by churches in South America.

Last and not least is the argument that all reform solidifies to become the status quo which must be challenged by the next generation. The Church, being an institution, is always in need of reform. The Old Testament bears out this truth— the institution which bore the responsibility for spiritual enlivenment was always falling into the trap of all human organisations, maintaining itself for itself, and was always in need of prophets calling for change. And it is never the holders of power who see what change is necessary; it is those on the periphery, the dissenters, who have the insight.

These are reasons for dissenters to try to stay and work for change. If they do, one of the major problems they face is that while the Church is clearly a multimillion dollar organisation run in ways that are not unlike the ways of corporations —with investments, financial interests, employees, legal sections, public relations, news services, and executives—it wants to maintain the image of a spiritual body which is somehow above the marketplace, is guided by God, and is a sacred community of believers. There is explicit teaching that everything the Church does is guided by the infallible word of God, the Bible, and by prayer and spiritual leaders with God's authority. The Church, that is, the institution and its members, is the Body of Christ and the hierarchy represent his head.

That's pretty difficult to argue against, as many have found to their detriment in the regular heretic hunts through centuries. It leaves the ordinary members, the 'consumer' in the parish, in a catch-22. If you raise an issue such as the ordination of women, you are told it is matter of doctrine and of the unquestionable word of God; on the other hand, matters in some cases are decided in a party political parliament, a synod, which rivals our Australian federal parliament for its lobbying, number-crunching and politicking.

Again and again, attempts to make Church governments more open have come to grief. Those who hold power in the Church are as loathe to forfeit it as any who hold power outside the Church. But the Church is an institution and the members of that institution, the 'citizens' of the institution, should have the same rights as all citizens. The Church, the *ecclesia*, should be what that word says: a gathering of citizens to decide their own future. We have the right to real participation in decision making and to seek change and growth in this organisation.

(Source: "Balaam's Ass", Sydney MOW, February 1990, adapted.)

Ali Wurm:

Sexuality and the Gospel of Love

A s Christians, we believe that Jesus makes all of us whole. All of us are loved and accepted by God. As Christians, we are baptised into a new community in which all members are called to partake equally in the freedom God has given us. This is the good news, but the Church says that this only applies to some people.

At present, women are not accepted as whole human beings

in the Church. Nor are homosexuals. The Church says to homosexuals: "We accept you, but we don't accept any expression of your sexuality"; "God loves you and accepts you, but any sexual relationship you are part of is sinful"; "You can only love God by being celibate or by converting to heterosexuality". In this way the Church marginalises and oppresses homosexuals.

Jesus says to us that the most important thing in life is to love God and to try to love our neighbour as ourselves, which implies loving ourselves. Any relationship has the potential to be creative or destructive, to be life-giving or to take life away. Any relationship can be sinful (destructive) or loving. This applies to friendships, marriages and lover relationships.

The gospel, or good news, is that God gives us love as a gift—regardless of our colour, age, sex or sexual orientation. God intends us to share this gift with others, and for many people a part of love is its sexual expression in a physically intimate way. Heterosexual people do not have a monopoly on love, or on what is right. Any truly loving relationship is right.

We are all different and each of us is unique. God's creation is beautiful and diverse. This diversity adds richness to life. Life would be extremely dull if we were all the same. Diversity helps us to survive as human beings in a changing world, and to find new possibilities. Some people are heterosexual, some are bisexual and others are homosexual. Some choose celibacy for their whole life and others choose celibacy for periods of their life. We all need to be where we are and to do what is right for us.

I believe that homosexuality is, for some people, just as valid an expression of love as heterosexuality is for others. What I do see as sinful is that people should claim that the only right way to live is their way, when that way includes denying others (homosexuals, for example) their identity as loving, sexual people.

Clearly, as Christians we need to be open to the present living God. Truth is not confined to the Bible or to the Church. God is continually revealing new truths to us, which include what the Church is to be. The ordination of women will be a powerful symbol of mutual acceptance of men and women in the Church. I believe that it is vital that we also express our full acceptance of homosexuals if we are to be a truly loving church.

(Source: MOW Newsletter, September 1987.)

Heather Thomson:

Spitting on the Sea

One Sunday afternoon, a woman rolled up her sleeping mat, collected together her plate and cup and a few other personal belongings, and set off up the road towards the nearby village of Niama. She had heard talk of a meeting, a woman's meeting, that was to be held in Niama and that women from the surrounding villages were invited to come. As she walked along, with the mountains on one side of her and the sea on the other, she thought of all that she had heard about the meeting.

It was to last a whole week, and for once the Government Officers who were running the meeting were coming to their villages, down the road from the town, across the mountains and down the west coast road to their place. A three-hour journey on a good day.

She had heard on the radio that every day they would learn something different, and that she could go back to her village and teach her women's group all that she had heard.

On one day they would have a Health Talk. The Health Officer would teach them how to care for their children so that they could grow up strong: how they must not leave coconut shells upturned around the village where they will collect water and breed mosquitoes and spread malaria: how they must wash their hands before touching food and keep their place of toilet away from the village.

Another day would be on sewing, using the hand-turned

143

machines that many women's groups had purchased with a government grant. They would learn how to draft patterns from a pair of child's shorts for smaller and larger sizes; how to patch and mend so that their clothes would last longer.

They would have a day on cooking where she and the others would learn how to prepare meals that were good for their health and they'd try foods they hadn't tried before. Someone would show them how to make an oven out of a drum and they'd bake yeast-breads and cakes in the drum-oven.

She had heard, too, that some women's groups were enterprising and, like the group in Niama, ran a Trade Store in their village. They would learn at the meeting about basic bookkeeping and how to run a small business. This could be good for the whole village. Basic supplies of food were available in the Trade Store: clothes, kerosene for their lamps and dairy products which were kept in a kerosene refrigerator. Villagers did not have to take the long trip to town so often, as the women's group hired a truck once a month to get supplies.

The woman walking to Niama thought how important all these things were. In her village she was president of her women's group and she knew that if they did not have something good planned for their weekly meetings they would just sit around and sew and gossip. And that was no good. It was destructive. There was so much, she thought, that could be done to improve their own lives and the welfare of the whole village.

On the last day of the women's meeting they would learn of things they could make and build to improve their conditions. For example, she knew that the women of Niama had a brick club-house built for them by the students of a nearby Technical Training College. It was the only brick building in the village. All the others were bush material. On top of the brick club-house was a roof of corrugated iron.

Around the roof was a gutter, with a down-pipe, and this pipe led into a water tank. Thus the women's group in Niama had supplied their village with fresh water. They no longer had to walk each day over the hill and down into the valley for water. But their gutters had rusted. At the meeting they

144

would learn about plastic pipes, and how to cover a water tank with cement so that it would be longer lasting and not rust away quickly with the salt air from the sea.

All the villages were by the sea, linked together by the road that the woman walked along. As she slept that night on the floor of the brick club-house in Niama, she heard the sound of the sea lapping onto the shore, the same sea sounds that she had heard every night since she had been born.

The next morning when they got up to begin their week-long meeting, the women saw that the sea was grey and restless, and a heavy rain fell and a strong wind blew all day, stronger than they had ever known. The women huddled together under the shelter that was built for their meeting and heard their health talk.

On the second day of the meeting, the heavy rain still fell, the strong wind still blew and the sea began to rise. The woman said to herself: "This is a curse".

On the third day of the meeting the heavy rain continued to fall, the strong wind still blew and the sea rose so much that it was moving into the nearest house of the village, frightening those who lived there and threatening to destroy the meeting. The woman said to the people of Niama: "Where are your magic men?" They answered: "They are not here. They are gone. They are visiting another village."

"All right", said the woman, "then I will have to work out myself who has put this curse upon our meeting."

She went away for a while, then returned, saying: "Three men have put a curse upon us. They are jealous of our meeting. They are angry that we are here and not at our own place, cooking and caring for our husbands and children."

"There are three of them", she said, "and only one of me, so I may not have the power, but I will see what I can do."

The woman went away again and made preparations, and on the afternoon of the third day she walked down to the edge of the sea, and stood alone in front of it. She spoke words to the sea and spat lime on it.

That evening the wind abated. The next morning the clouds were gone, and the sun shone on a calm and peaceful day and the sea had retreated to its proper place.

145

Some women said: "It was magic." Others said: "It was just coincidence. The weather got better, that's all."

(Source: MOW Newsletter, Autumn 1989.)

Sister Angela of Stroud:

Interview by Elaine Lindsay

Are the Church and God about the same thing?

You read Hildegard of Bingen, and she's talking about the greening God. She's leaping over all boundaries of descriptions of God. But then you look at the Church, and it has got itself boxed in. Frankly, I think Jesus, if he were here now, would say of the Church, "What's this?" It isn't buildings and yet we think of it as buildings, and as hierarchy. We think of parochial Church councils, of keeping the fabric intact. To me, this is totally secondary. What the Church is, what God is on about, is you and me. So many people come here and say, "We don't want to be married in church, we want to be married in the bush." And I say, "Well, God's there—why not?"

But then there is the mystery of the Body of Christ, the Church. I think the Church has to get back the poverty of St Clare and St Francis, to own the simplicity of what Christ was teaching. Christ wasn't a Christian. Christianity formed after Christ. Christ wasn't a priest. People say this is being simplistic, but it isn't. It's that poverty of soul that goes to the heart of what Christianity is about. It's the truth that shines out of a child's eye, a happy child's eyes. That is God to me and it is part of the Church's structure.

This monastery is part of that structure, but we are on the periphery. All religious are on the periphery because we've totally given ourselves to God and that oversteps all barriers. Some of my best friends are Catholic women religious because there's no difference in our dedication or our outlook. We get divided because the Church says "You don't communicate with this sister because she's Anglican." Eventually it's going to rest between me and God, isn't it? My conscience says we're breaking down barriers by communicating together. This is what the Clares and the religious are trying to do—to live out this freedom of the Spirit and this poverty of soul. God didn't put up barriers between people.

And this is where I'm fascinated with the feminine creativity of women Hebrew scholars who are retranslating the creation story. The woman isn't second to the man. There's a mistranslation of the original Hebrew and it's gone on for fear of rocking the boat. That's not honest. We have to get back to the simplicity of looking at what we're on about. I think that's what St Clare and St Francis did: they shook the Church, then built it up again because they said there's something more in life than this great panoply of state.

What would a free Church be like?

I can see why there have to be certain guidelines for what one believes. There are an awful lot of sects whose theology, to me, is totally haywire. There have to be guidelines and that's where structure comes in. I'm not saying that all structure has to go, but I think structures have to change.

It's not really a case of whether women are going to be ordained priests or consecrated bishops—it is whether there's a pope who is a woman, and when there is no differentiation. The structures will change because women look differently at them than men.

This is where we're going to see great change in the future. You think of a woman: she conceives a child, she bears that child for nine months and she builds up a link with that child within her womb. She strokes her belly and the little baby moves over to feel that rubbing on its back, and if she does it on the other side, it goes over to the other side. The child is born and straight away there's that link with the mother. From the moment that child is conceived the woman is planning, she has to prepare for its coming. As soon as it's born, there's the feeding, the clothing, the washing and the ironing.

147

More and more children come, and my God, she's a brilliant lady. I think woman are fantastic people. The men haven't got to do it. They say they're out hitting the animals on the head to get a bit of tucker.

But we're a long way from those days now. What I'm saying is that, as far as the Church is concerned, when you get women involved in parishes, having to feel their way in the system, that system is already changing. A woman, if she's given a job looking after the children and the old people in the parish, straight away says "Well, the children really need the old people because they've got wisdom, and the old people need the young people because they give them new life." She links them together, doesn't she? But the system doesn't do that; it keeps them totally separate in their separate boxes.

Women don't think that way, women aren't hierarchical thinkers, women cross the board the whole time, they're planners. I think they're fantastic because they're using their creativity from the moment they wake up in the morning and even during the night, in their dreams. It's not to say that men haven't got this creativity too.

We've got to show the men that, OK, they're stronger physically, but, my God, that's the only thing they're stronger at.

I think it's the women who have really moved creation along. So I think the Church is going to change, it must change. The first woman diocesan bishop is already consecrated in New Zealand and there's the assistant bishop in America—and they're the first. It's moving and nothing is going to stop it because I believe that the whole creativity thing is just coming out. Politically, what's happening in Europe and Russia now, what's happening in South America, what happened when Corey Aquino first got to power—to me this is the creativity thing, people banding together in order to demand freedom of being. And again, it is a feminine thing.

The conservative process is also being undermined. Ten years ago you didn't mix across denominational lines, let alone countries. And here's Russia asking the West for help. You couldn't have thought of that even last year! This is God to me. This is God saying, "You're going to destroy this planet

148

if you don't get together and think big together." This is God planning to save this jewel because there is no other planet that is like earth. To me this is a gift we have to take responsibility for. And so we come back to St Francis and St Clare, we move full circle all the time.

I am totally committed to this way of life because I totally believe in it, because I think it is saying something for this moment in time. I see the whole feminine thing working when men can own their feminine—I've seen the men who do opening out in the most gorgeous ways.

And the women have to own their feminine. It's about saying: "I am going to be totally feminine, I am going to look feminine, be feminine, think feminine, because that's my strength", its not about trying to ape a man. I think when the Church gets onto this level, and stops being afraid of women and creativity, things are going to really hum.

The planet will survive. I know they only give us twenty years, but I believe we're brilliant. God created us to be the carers of this jewel and to learn about God. I can see the whole of our Christian Bible as a picture of what went wrong. God created this creature in the image of God, and that image was to be God. To be God gives you the power to turn your back, doesn't it? Which is what happened. And our Bible is really trying to say, "For God's sake, turn around and do what I'm asking you."

There's an element in you that is not God. Life was not meant to be a drudgery, you made it a drudgery by turning your back on life. But God designed you to dance, *to dance!* Scientists are now telling us that the whole cosmos is humming. We hear about hydrogen clouds: all these brilliant colours moving at different speeds. And the music, *the music!* This is God. If we all started thinking of a dancing God, what a difference!

I have a game I play when I have to go to town. The crowd pours towards me and I try to meet people's eyes. Occasionally somebody does a double take. They meet my eye and I'm smiling at them and they smile back. They won't forget that smile. What if the whole word were full of laughter, of singing, of dancing, of smiling at people? Wouldn't be bad, would it?

This is part of what St Clare was about and it's what I think I'm about. I just find it totally exciting. Life's marvellous.

If my cancer flares up again and I hop off, that's OK, because I'm going into what is totally gorgeous. I'm totally convinced of that too. So were Francis and Clare. You know this life doesn't end. Life is going on, no doubt about that. I've got the freedom that comes from being a Clare. Our enclosure gives us that freedom to think big, to dance big, to grow and to grow things, to talk. People think I talk nonsense about these sorts of things and they say to me, "Angela, come off it, life's not like that." But life is like that, if we could only see it.

What about when people come to see you in their bereavement?

I'll instance my father. My parents were a devoted couple. My mother died when about 82. My father was a doctor and he nursed her through her last years and it was fairly dicey, because she'd lost her memory. But when she died, it was as though a little bit of him had gone. He felt totally bereft. We used to talk about my mother (I think it's very important to talk about the person who has died because the soul of that person is not dead, but is caught up in the mystery of God). After two years my Father said "Have I been a peculiar old man?" And I said, "No, you haven't been; you've been a very sad old man." I own that sadness.

We're taught that God is love. Now the love that God put into you you've shared in marriage with another person. Together you share this love of God on a Christian level, and together you go towards God. You remain autonomous—it's not a business of possessing each other, it's the joy of saying, "Come on, let's do it together. It's going to be fun." That's the ideal of marriage. When I talk to people I think it is important to say that we come in alone and we go out alone. The person whom we linked up with in love is there, waiting for us to get there.

I always remember the story of one of our sisters who was to come out with us when we came to Australia, but she died of lung cancer. We nursed her through it and right near the end she came to for the second last time. "Oh, I'm still here", she said, "I thought I'd gone that time." She drifted off again and then she opened her eyes, she focussed on somebody we couldn't see and said, "Why, hullo, hullo, hullo!" She looked back at us and said "Goodbye", and she went. I tell that story because it shows that there is an on-goingness and there is a love that nothing can separate us from. That's what Paul meant, I think, when he said in Romans: "Neither height, nor depth, nor principalities, nor powers, nor death, nor life can separate us" (cf. Romans 8:38-9).

Nothing can separate us from that love of God because God is in us, and God is all love. Therefore, those people whom we loved and who have died, while we don't see them, they are in our hearts. Nothing will separate us. We're going to go there, we're going to be part of them and they're going to be part of us forever. That love can never be separated. I think it's in the scriptures. I've certainly experienced it in my own personal life. When you nearly die you get a glimpse of other things. When I had a vision of death, the people were all balls of light. We're all balls of light at that point and we'll certainly know those we love, but how, or in what way? Love is a fulfilling, so there's going to be a fulfilling. I haven't any doubt about it.

Irene McCormack, RSJ

An extract from a letter written by Sister McCormack dated the seventeenth day of July, 1990. Irene McCormack was killed in Peru, from where this letter was written, on the twenty-first day of May, 1991. In this and other letters she writes of the Eucharist and its meaning for her.

In our capacity of 'acting parish priest', May was an especially busy month, with many fiesta 'Masses' in Huasahuasi itself and in lots of the villages. In a couple of places the celebration is in honour of Mary, but the principal devotion is to the *'Cruz de Mayo'* or *'El Senor de Mayo'*. I guess in the Church calendar we're accustomed to, the closest parallel is the feast of the Triumph of the Cross.

The format followed was this—a journey of 1 hour to 1½ hours by Jeep, mostly upwards; choir practice on arrival while the secretary inscribed those for baptisms; the liturgy, procession, baptisms (my record for one day is ten); dancing, and in some places lunch, or a cup of warm milk and dry biscuits.

Am not sure if it's a characteristic of my Australianness (that we 'do' first and 'theorise' afterwards, if at all), or of my Josephiteness (brought up on Mary McKillop's saying, "Never see a need without seeking a remedy"), or my 'threeness' on the Enneagram!, but in and from the doing in recent months I find in myself a new appreciation, a new conviction along with a new anger and resentment about two particular aspects of Eucharist and ministry.

In response to the General Chapter challenge to update our study of the Eucharist, I've been reading Tad Guzie's book *Jesus and the Eucharist* and we've recently had two days with the Lima sisters, reflecting on this theme, so I'm motivated to strive to express where I'm at—but first back to experience.

A few weeks ago I celebrated with an extended family a *'Misa de honras'* for the grandfather, dead many years. Note I've given up trying to use the terms 'paraliturgy' or 'liturgy of the word' or any of the 'excuses' the official Church uses to deny collaborative ministry its rightful place with women and married lay people. I used to try to do the 'right' thing and correct people when they came asking us to celebrate their *'Misas'*. I've become convinced that they are closer to the truth and were 'freeing' me to exercise Eucharistic ministry amongst them.

Now, how do I translate *'Misa de honras'*? *'Misa'* speaks for itself—'Mass of Honour'. There is, of course, the element of praying for the fullness of eternal life for the person, but I suspect it is more a way of giving thanks for the life of the person and keeping his/her memory alive to the family.

After the 'Mass', I was invited to lunch—about 60 present. A simple meal, the usual fiesta fare, was served—first course a potato dish, next boiled rice, a little meat and a picante sauce, finally a large bowl of maize soup. Before the food arrived, as is customary, we drank beer, and as usual passed around the bottle and one glass with a 'ritual' receiving and giving. When I first encountered this custom in Lima, I thought it was just a way of coping with a shortage of glasses, but soon learnt that it's not that, but rather a symbol of friendship/fellowship. The last mouthful poured on the ground, my hygiene-dominated background made me presume was a means of cleansing the glass, but discovered it came from giving honour to the *'pachamama'*—'mother earth'. Thus sitting next to the old grandmother and seeing her pouring out a little each round into a container on the floor in front of her, in a place of honour, I presumed this was the same tradition. On asking her about it, she gently explained that, no, it was for the 'dead one'.

Reflecting on the experience afterwards, I felt much more in touch with what the Last Supper and the Eucharist were and are on about. When Jesus said "Do this in memory of me", he couldn't have been emphasising the "do this", i.e., have a meal—which of course for the Jews always had ritual connotations, including prayers and blessings over each kind of food, the breaking of bread and sharing the cup—as the apostles had always done this and for sure would continue doing so. Thus if it was pointless to command them "to do this"—the emphasis then had to be on the second part--"in memory of me", i.e., when you go on doing what you've so often done together, you'll be *remembering me* in what you are *doing*.

It seems to me, therefore, that the preoccupation of our Church leaders with power and control over who can celebrate the Eucharist, who can and who can't receive the Eucharist, is right up the creek. It's a contradiction to be talking about a 'sacred meal', and have to sit and watch, not participate—quite apart from the lack of the atmosphere of a fellowship meal, or lack of basic symbolism when only one person drinks from the cup and we use a tasteless wafer in place of bread.

Of course, too, our preoccupation with the only reality being the scientific, the empirical, makes it hard for us to accept the

153

validity of symbolism. Not only is it a contradiction to the proclamation of Jesus that there is no distinction between male and female, but a lack of appreciation of the plight of villagers like ours all over the world, that our Church continues denying its official ministry, that is by nature 'communion'. As we in our little Christian communities, high up in the Andes, gather in memory of Jesus, there is no power or authority on earth that can convince me that Jesus is not personally present. I feel grateful that these months on end without the 'official Mass' and in a culture where I'm experiencing new symbols, have gifted me with a new appreciation of Eucharist.

(Source: Compass: A Review of Topical Theology, vol. 25(4), 1991 pp. 33–5.)